W9-AUU-353

SCOTT COUNTY LIBRARY
SAVAGE MN 55378

dk online

insect

LONDON, NEW YORK, MELBOURNE,
MUNICH, and DELHI

Senior Editor Clare Lister | Senior Art Editor Jim Green
Weblink Editors Niki Foreman, John Bennett | Designers Jacqui Swan, Nicola Harrison
Cartography Simon Mumford | Illustrators Mark Longworth, Robin Hunter

Managing Editor Linda Esposito | Managing Art Editor Diane Thistlethwaite

Digital Development Manager Fergus Day | Picture Research Frances Vargo
DTP Co-ordinator Tony Cutting | Picture Librarians Sarah Mills, Kate Ledwith

Jacket Copywriter Adam Powley | Production Emma Hughes
Jacket Editor Mariza O'Keeffe | Jacket Designer Neal Cobourne

Publishing Managers Andrew Macintyre, Caroline Buckingham | Art Director Simon Webb
Consultant Dr George McGavin,
Oxford University Museum of Natural History

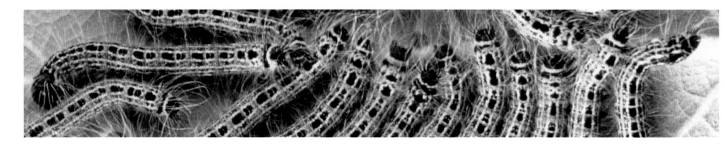

First American hardback edition published in 2005.
This edition first published in 2007.

Published in the United States by DK Publishing, Inc.
375 Hudson Street, New York, New York 10014

07 08 09 10 9 8 7 6 5 4 3 2 1

Copyright © 2005, 2007 Dorling Kindersley Limited

Google™ is a trademark of Google Technology Inc.

All rights reserved under International and Pan-American Copyright Conventions.
No part of this publication may be reproduced, stored
in a retrieval system, or transmitted in any form or by any means,
electronic, mechanical, photocopying, recording, or otherwise,
without the prior written permission of the copyright owner.
Published in Great Britain by Dorling Kindersley Limited.

A Cataloging-in-Publication record for this book is available from the Library of Congress.

ISBN 978-0-75662-294-7

Color reproduction by Media Development and Printing, UK
Printed in China by Toppan Printing Co. (Shenzen) Ltd

Discover more at
www.dk.com

dk online

insect

Written by **David Burnie**

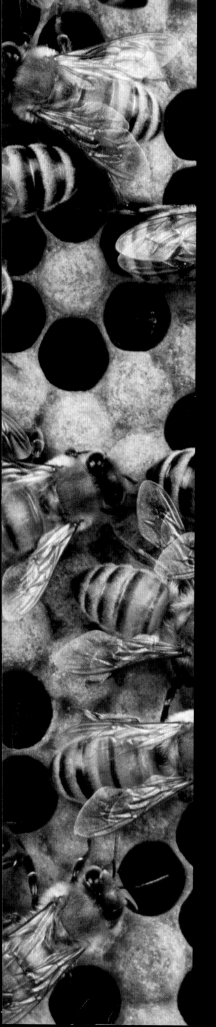

CONTENTS

How to use the Web site

DK online Insect has its own Web site, created by DK and Google™. When you look up a subject in the book, the article gives you key facts and displays a keyword that links you to extra information online. Just follow these easy steps.

http://www.insect.dkonline.com

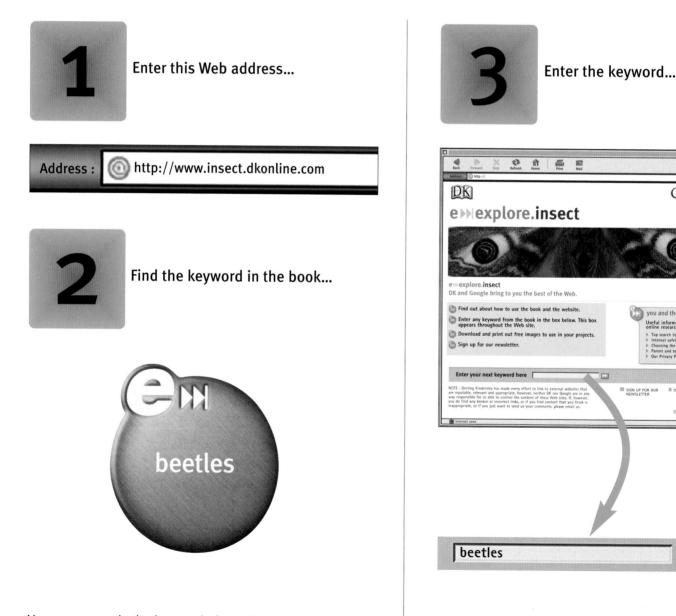

1 Enter this Web address...

Address : http://www.insect.dkonline.com

2 Find the keyword in the book...

beetles

3 Enter the keyword...

beetles

You can use only the keywords from the book to search on our Web site for the specially selected DK/Google links.

Be safe while you are online:

- Always get permission from an adult before connecting to the internet.

- Never give out personal information about yourself.

- Never arrange to meet someone you have talked to online.

- If a site asks you to log in with your name or email address, ask permission from an adult first.

- Do not reply to emails from strangers—tell an adult.

Parents: Dorling Kindersley actively and regularly reviews and updates the links. However, content may change. Dorling Kindersley is not responsible for any site but its own. We recommend that children are supervised while online, that they do not use Chat Rooms, and that filtering software is used to block unsuitable material.

4 Click on your chosen link...

5 Download fantastic pictures...

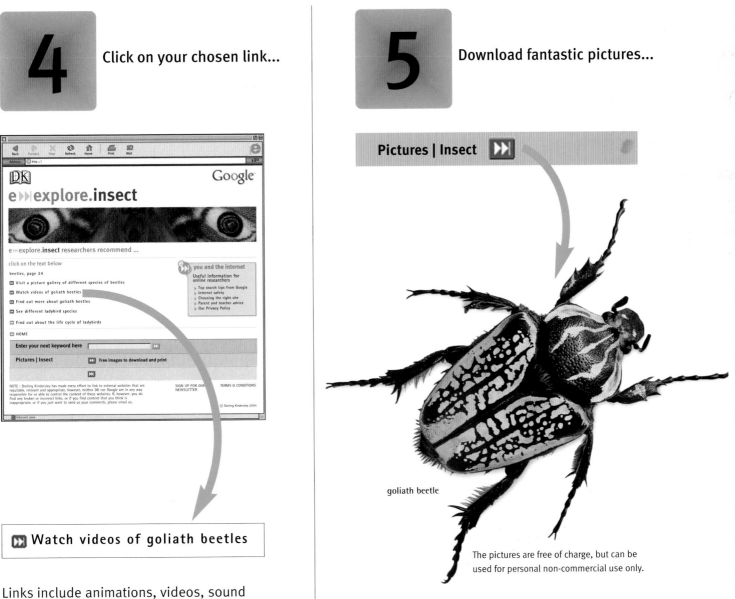

Pictures | Insect

goliath beetle

The pictures are free of charge, but can be used for personal non-commercial use only.

📹 Watch videos of goliath beetles

Links include animations, videos, sound buttons, virtual tours, interactive quizzes, databases, timelines, and realtime reports.

Go back to the book for your next subject...

Club-shaped antenna typical of a butterfly

INSECT WORLD

Insects are amazingly successful animals. They outnumber humans by over a billion times, and they make up over a half of all the animal species on Earth. So far, scientists have identified more than one million species, and they think that even more will be discovered. Scientists classify insects into groups called orders. Within each order, the insects share the same key features. Seven of the major orders are bees, wasps, and ants; flies; beetles; butterflies and moths; dragonflies and damselflies; crickets and grasshoppers; and true bugs.

Forewing links to hind wing with a row of tiny hooks

Well-developed eyes

Single pair of wings

▲ TWO-WINGED FLIES
Unlike most flying insects, flies, including this house fly, have just one pair of wings. Instead of hind wings, they have a pair of small knobs called halteres, which help to stabilize them during flight. Find out more about flies on pages 40–41.

Jaws used by males for fighting

Furlike scales keep in body heat

▲ BEES
Bees, wasps, and ants have a body with a narrow waist, and two pairs of filmy wings. Many of them can sting. Some of these insects live alone, but many form permanent groups called colonies. Bees carry out vital work in nature by pollinating flowers. Without them, many plants would be unable to make seeds. Find out more about bees, wasps, and ants on pages 76–77.

Elytra (hard forewings) meet in a line down the back

INSECT SECRETS OF SUCCESS

TOUGH BODY CASE Instead of having bones, insects have an exoskeleton (body case). This case makes them strong for their size, and it also helps to stop them from drying out. This means that insects can survive in some of the driest places on Earth.

SMALL SIZE Compared to vertebrates (animals with backbones) insects are usually small. This allows them to live in all kinds of places that larger animals cannot use. Small animals also eat less, so they are better at surviving when food is scarce.

FLIGHT When insects are fully grown, most of them can fly. For insects, flight is a huge advantage, because it makes it easier to find food, and to spread. Most insects do not fly far, but some travel long distances to search for somewhere to breed.

RAPID REPRODUCTION Compared to mammals, insects breed quickly, and they often have enormous families. When the weather is good and there is lots of food, their numbers can multiply by thousands in the space of just a few weeks.

VARIED DIETS Individual insects often eat just one kind of food. But as a whole, insects eat almost anything, from living plants and animals to dead remains. These varied diets mean that there are many opportunities for insects to feed.

Strong legs for clambering around

Hooked feet for climbing trees

▲ BEETLES
With nearly 400,000 different species, beetles make up the largest order of insects. Beetles come in a range of shapes and sizes, but they all have hard forewings, called elytra, which fit over their hind wings like a case. This order includes heavyweights such as stag beetles, which are equipped with a pair of fearsome antlers. Find out more about beetles on pages 24–25.

Wing surface *covered in colored scales*

Forewings *are larger than the hind wings*

GRASSHOPPERS ▶

Many insects have strong legs or well-developed wings, but crickets and grasshoppers have both. They usually move around by jumping, but if they need to travel in a hurry, most of them can fly. Their forewings are narrow and leathery, but their hind wings are much thinner, and can open out like fans. Find out more about crickets and grasshoppers on pages 56–57.

Hind wings *provide most of the power for flight*

Narrow forewings *often have camouflaged markings*

Large thorax *contains flight muscles*

◀ BUTTERFLIES

The large order of butterflies and moths includes some of the world's most beautiful insects, such as this European swallowtail. Butterflies and moths vary hugely in shape, size, and color, but they all share one key feature—their bodies and wings are covered in tiny scales. Find out more about butterflies and moths on pages 68–69.

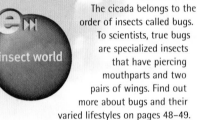

insect world

TRUE BUGS ▶

The cicada belongs to the order of insects called bugs. To scientists, true bugs are specialized insects that have piercing mouthparts and two pairs of wings. Find out more about bugs and their varied lifestyles on pages 48–49.

DRAGONFLIES ▶

With their long bodies and stiff wings, these insects search for food over water and open spaces. They have superb eyesight, and they feed on other insects, using their bristly legs to grab their prey. Find out more about this ancient order of insects on pages 30–31.

Long sticklike *abdomen gives a streamlined shape*

OTHER INSECT ORDERS

COCKROACHES
These nocturnal scavengers eat dead and decaying remains. Most live harmlessly in tropical forests, but a handful of species cause problems by infesting people's homes. Most cockroaches have wings, but the largest species—such as this Madagascan hissing cockroach—are wingless.

EARWIGS
With their distinctive pincers, earwigs are familiar garden insects all over the world. They can fly, but when they crawl around, their fan-shaped hind wings are folded up and hidden away. Earwigs use their pincers in self-defense and to capture their prey, such as aphids, mites, and fleas.

THE OLDEST INSECTS

About 300 million years ago, the first winged insects appeared. These prehistoric fliers included giant dragonflies, such as this one fossilized in limestone. Some prehistoric dragonflies had a 29 in (75 cm) wingspan, making them the largest flying insects of all time.

The earliest insectlike creatures date back nearly 400 million years ago. These insect relatives did not have wings, and they looked similar to tiny animals called springtails, which still exist today.

LACEWINGS
It is easy to see how lacewings get their name. Their wings are larger than their bodies and are covered by a network of delicate veins. Lacewings are nocturnal, and they often flutter around bright lights. They have small jaws, but are voracious predators of aphids and other small insects.

WHAT IS AN INSECT?

The world is full of small animals that scuttle around on lots of legs. They are known as arthropods, and they include all the world's insects, and also lots of insect look-alikes. It's easy to get these animals mixed up, unless you know what sets insects apart. Adult insects always have a three-part body, made up of the head, thorax, and abdomen, and they always have three pairs of legs. They are also the only arthropods that have wings. Young insects can be trickier to recognize, because they change shape as they grow up. This change is called metamorphosis.

insect world

Tibia of middle leg

Tarsus (foot) of middle leg

Femur of middle leg

Coxa attaches the hind leg to the thorax

Tibia of hindleg

Femur of hindleg

Tarsus (foot) of hindleg

Hindwings are folded away when not in use

EXPLODED INSECT ►
This jewel beetle has been dismantled to show how an insect's body is made up. Its body is divided into three main sections: the head, the thorax, and the abdomen. The head contains the brain and carries two compound eyes. The thorax contains muscles that the beetle uses for moving. It is the part where the legs and wings are attached. The abdomen is the largest part of all three. It contains the reproductive system and the beetle's intestines. A hard body case, called an exoskeleton, covers the whole of the beetle's body, including its eyes.

Abdomen is made of hard segments that meet at flexible joints

INSECT LOOK-ALIKES

SPIDER
Unlike insects, spiders have four pairs of legs. They also have only two body sections: a front part, called the cephalothorax, and the rear part, or abdomen. Like all arthropods, spiders have an exoskeleton, but it is often thin and covered with silky hairs. Spiders do not change shape as they grow up.

TICK
Ticks are closely related to spiders and also have four pairs of legs. They climb onto animals to feed on their blood—the one shown here has swollen up after a lengthy meal. Mites belong to the same arthropod order as ticks, but are much smaller and can often be seen only with a microscope.

WOODLOUSE
The woodlouse is one of the few crustaceans that lives on land. Crustaceans include crabs and shrimps, and most live in freshwater or the sea. Crustaceans get their name from their heavily armored exoskeleton, which surrounds them like a crust. Unlike insects, they often have over a dozen pairs of legs.

CENTIPEDE
A centipede's body has lots of segments, and each one carries a single pair of legs. Some species have more than 300 legs, although most have far fewer. Centipedes' bodies are flat, which helps them to wriggle through crevices in search of their prey. They kill with poison claws, located on each side of the head.

Tibia *of front leg*

Tarsus (foot)
ends in two claws

Femur *of
front leg*

Antennae *sense air
currents and smells*

Muscle-filled thorax *is
covered by a hard plate*

Coxa *of
front leg*

Compound
eye *contains
many small
units packed
together*

Coxa *attaches the
leg to the thorax*

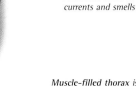

Magnified
beetle
exoskeleton
*showing
tufts of hair*

◄ EXOSKELETON
An insect's exoskeleton
covers its entire body.
It often looks shiny and smooth,
but it is covered with microscopic
structures that help its owner to survive. These
structures can include scales, hooks, hairs, or even
long threads that look like yarn. The surface of
the exoskeleton is usually coated in wax, which gives
insects their glossy sheen. Wax works like a waterproof
barrier. It helps to stop an insect's body moisture
from evaporating into the air.

*Front wings
form hard covers
called elytra*

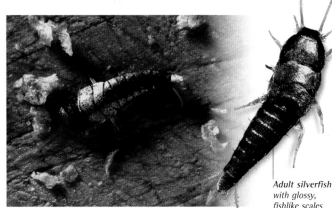

*Adult silverfish
with glossy,
fishlike scales*

▲ YOUNG SILVERFISH
Most insects change shape as they grow up. The changes happen when they molt
(shed their skin), so that they can grow. Most insects shed their skin
a set number of times—after that, they do not grow any more. Primitive insects
called silverfish are one of the few exceptions to this rule. They keep molting
throughout their lives, and they hardly change shape at all. Silverfish do not
have wings, and they are covered in silvery scales. They first appeared more
than 350 million years ago and have changed very little since.

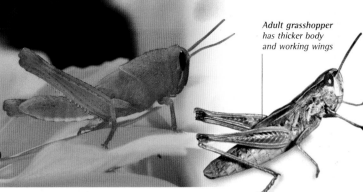

*Adult grasshopper
has thicker body
and working wings*

▲ GRASSHOPPER NYMPH
Grasshoppers are insects that change gradually as they grow up. A young
grasshopper (nymph) looks similar to its parents—the main difference is
that it does not have a working reproductive system or wings. Each time the
grasshopper molts, it becomes more like an adult. After the last molt, its
wings are fully formed, and it is ready to breed. This kind of change is called
incomplete metamorphosis.

*Adult crane
fly with
slender
wings*

▲ CRANE FLY GRUB
A crane fly grub, or larva, does not have any legs, and looks
nothing like its parents. For several months, it eats and feeds, but
hardly changes shape. Then something drastic happens. It stops feeding and
enters a resting stage called a pupa. During this stage, its body is broken down
and an adult one is built up in its place. Once the adult is ready, it emerges and
prepares to breed. This kind of change is called complete metamorphosis.

INSECT HABITATS

Wherever you are in the world, insects are not far away. They live in every type of habitat on land, from steamy tropical rain forests to the darkness and silence of caves. Many insects grow up in freshwater, and plenty spend their adult lives there as well. Some insects live along the shore, and a few even skate over the surface of the waves. Only one habitat—the ocean depths—is entirely insect-free.

Slender body without wings

BRISTLETAIL

Long antennae for sensing food

▲ COASTS AND SEAS

The coast is a difficult place for insects. Many live in dunes or on clifftop grass, but very few can survive in places that get soaked by salty spray. Beach insects include bristletails, which scuttle among stones and rocks. Long-legged bugs called sea skaters are the only insects that live on the open sea.

INSECT HABITATS

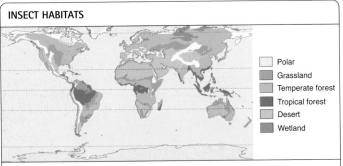

☐	Polar
☐	Grassland
☐	Temperate forest
☐	Tropical forest
☐	Desert
☐	Wetland

This map shows the world's main biomes (habitats). Biomes are living communities that have a particular mix of plants. For example, deserts have plants that are good at surviving drought, while rain forests have fast-growing evergreen trees. These plants provide food for the biome's animals. Grasslands, for example, are famous for their hoofed mammals: without grass, they could not survive.

Insects live in all the world's biomes, from the tropics to land close to the poles. In the tropics, it is always warm, so insects can stay busy throughout the year. Farther north and south, insect life comes and goes. They explode into life in spring and summer, but by the time winter comes, very few are on the move.

◀ GRASSLANDS

The most numerous grassland insects are termites and ants. They scour every inch of the surface for food, collecting seeds and leaves and carrying them back to their nests. Dung beetles are particularly useful in this habitat. They clear up the droppings that grazing mammals leave behind.

Armored head for protection

GRASSLAND TERMITE

▼ TEMPERATE WOODLANDS

Every spring, temperate woodlands burst into leaf, creating a gigantic banquet for insect life. Caterpillars chew their way through this tasty food, while predatory insects, such as hornets, harvest huge numbers of caterpillars and other grubs to feed to their young.

HORNET

Large eyes used for spotting prey

INSECTS INDOORS

Some insects normally live outside, but come indoors for food. These unwelcome visitors include the house fly, which settles on anything sugary, mopping it up with its spongelike tongue. Ants are also fond of things that taste sweet. If an ant finds sugary food, it spreads the news. Soon, hundreds more arrive to carry it outside.

Many insects accidentally wander indoors. But, for some, houses are a permanent habitat— one that provides warmth and food. Silverfish live in houses all over the world. They hide by day and come out after dark to feed on starchy foods. Cockroaches are more of a problem. They have much bigger appetites, and they breed very rapidly in warm conditions, making them hard to control.

HOUSE FLY

FRESHWATER ►

Lakes, rivers, ponds, and streams teem with insect life. Mosquito larvae feed on microscopic specks of food, but some freshwater insects, such as water bugs, are big enough to kill tadpoles and even small fish. On the water's surface pondskaters pounce on insects that have crash-landed, grabbing them before they have a chance to fly away.

Spiny front legs grip prey

GIANT WATER BUG

Flattened rear legs work like oars

CAVES AND MOUNTAINS ►

Caves are home to some unusual insects. Cave crickets are almost blind and use their extra-long antennae to find their way in the dark. Mountains are often cold and windswept, but many insects use them as a home. Beetles scavenge for food among rocks, while butterflies and bees pollinate flowers. High above the snowline, wingless scorpion flies scuttle around under the snow.

Plump, wingless body

CAVE CRICKET

Antennae can be much longer than body

e ▸▸

habitats

NAMIB DARKLING BEETLE

◄ DESERTS

Compared to many animals, insects are well suited to desert life. Some of them feed during the day, but many wait until after dark. Desert insects include hawk moths, ant lions, and giant crickets, as well as many kinds of ground-dwelling beetles. Some of these animals never have to drink, but this darkling beetle, from the Namib Desert, collects droplets of moisture from fog that rolls in from the sea.

Pale elytra reflect the sun's heat

◄ TROPICAL FORESTS

The world's tropical forests have more kinds of insects than all other habitats put together. They range from microscopic wasps to giant butterflies, like this Cairns birdwing, whose wings measure 11 in (28 cm) from tip to tip. In tropical forests, many bees and flies feed on flowers, while termites and beetles feast on rotting wood. Columns of army ants swarm over the floor, overpowering any other insects in their path.

Extra-large forewings with pointed tips

CAIRNS BIRDWING BUTTERFLY

LIFE IN A CASE

Humans and mice look very different, but we have an important feature in common. Human skeletons (called endoskeletons) are inside our bodies, and they are made of bone. The bones are connected by flexible joints, so that muscles can make them move. Insects are built in a completely different way. They also have joints, but their skeletons are outside their bodies, like a portable case. The case is made of curved plates and tubes, and it supports the insect's body from the outside. It is known as an exoskeleton.

anatomy

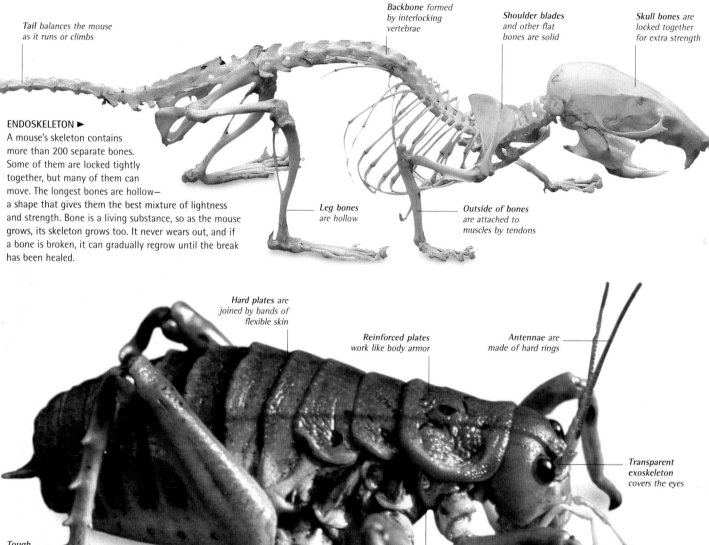

Tail balances the mouse as it runs or climbs

Backbone formed by interlocking vertebrae

Shoulder blades and other flat bones are solid

Skull bones are locked together for extra strength

ENDOSKELETON ►
A mouse's skeleton contains more than 200 separate bones. Some of them are locked tightly together, but many of them can move. The longest bones are hollow—a shape that gives them the best mixture of lightness and strength. Bone is a living substance, so as the mouse grows, its skeleton grows too. It never wears out, and if a bone is broken, it can gradually regrow until the break has been healed.

Leg bones are hollow

Outside of bones are attached to muscles by tendons

Hard plates are joined by bands of flexible skin

Reinforced plates work like body armor

Antennae are made of hard rings

Transparent exoskeleton covers the eyes

Tough spines

Underside of exoskeleton is softest part

▲ EXOSKELETON
Approximately the same size as a mouse, the giant weta has an exoskeleton rather than an endoskeleton. The case is strong and flexible and is made of a substance called chitin, which is topped by a layer of waterproof wax. The case covers the entire insect, protecting it and preventing it from drying out. Unlike a bony skeleton, this kind of casing cannot grow. As the weta grows, it periodically molts (sheds) its existing exoskeleton and grows a bigger one in its place.

Legs consist of hollow tubes with muscles inside

INFLATED INSECTS ►
Caterpillars have very thin exoskeletons, which is why they feel soft and spongy. These insects stay in shape because they are under pressure, like living balloons. Their body fluids press outward against their body case, stretching it and keeping it tight. The toughest parts of a caterpillar's skeleton are its jaws, because they are used for constant feeding on plant tissues.

Body fluids press outward

Thin exoskeleton resists internal pressure

Reinforced jaws for chewing leaves

Rear prolegs are softer than front legs and do not have joints

Prolegs cling to stems and leaves

Small front legs with flexible joints

Black and yellow are typical warning colors

Inflatable horns give off a strong smell

▲ CHEMICAL COLORS
An insect's color usually comes from its exoskeleton, or from body layers just beneath it. This swallowtail caterpillar has bright warning colors—a sign to birds and other predators that it has a bad taste. The colors are produced by chemical pigments (substances found in plants and animals). Caterpillars and other insects often get pigments from the plants that they eat.

IRIDESCENT COLORS ►
A morpho butterfly's blue color is produced by microscopic ridges on its wings. When sunlight falls on them, they reflect it in a special way. The light is diffracted, making the blue part of light stand out. This kind of color is called iridescence. Unlike pigment colors, iridescent colors change if you look at the insect from different angles. In dim light they look completely black.

Ridges on wing scales reflect the blue part of sunlight

Morpho's color appears to change as its wings beat

▲ SCALES AND HAIRS
Many insects have a smooth and shiny surface, but butterflies and moths are completely covered with tiny scales. Their wing scales overlap like tiles on a roof, and they often contain pigments that give them bright colors. Insects do not have real hair, but many have fine filaments that look like hair or fur. Caterpillars use their filaments for self-defense.

▲ COATS OF WAX
Magnified more than 30 times, this aphid looks as though it is covered in snow. The snow is actually wax that oozes out from tiny glands in the aphid's exoskeleton. The wax helps to stop the aphid from drying out, and it also makes it harder for parasites to attack. All insects have a waxy coating on their body surface.

EXTRA PROTECTION

Hanging beneath a twig, this bagworm caterpillar is hidden in a case made from leaves. The case works like an extra skin, protecting the caterpillar and its soft exoskeleton. Male moths leave the case to mate, but females remain inside the bag to lay their eggs.

Bagworm caterpillars are not the only insects to build themselves extra protection. Caddisfly larvae make themselves mobile homes, which they carry around underwater.

INSIDE INSECTS

An insect's internal organs do the same work as ours, but in different ways. For example, insects do not have lungs. Instead, oxygen enters their bodies through tiny tubes, called tracheae, which reach all of their cells. An insect's heart is long and narrow, and it runs just beneath its back. Unlike our blood, insect blood does not carry oxygen, and it is yellowish-green instead of red. Insects have brains in their heads, but they also have minibrains elsewhere. That is why an insect can keep kicking, even when a predator has turned most of it into a meal.

BODY SYSTEMS ▶

This cutaway of a bumble bee shows the major systems that keep its body working. The nervous system controls the muscles and gathers information from the eyes and other sense organs. The circulatory system stores water and fends off infection, while the respiratory system delivers oxygen. The digestive system breaks down food and absorbs it to give the bee energy.

◀ AIR SUPPLY

This photograph shows a single air tube (trachea), magnified thousands of times. Each trachea starts as a single tube, but then divides into ultrafine branches that spread deep into an insect's body. Oxygen diffuses (spreads) through the tubes from the air outside and into the insect's cells. At the same time, carbon dioxide waste diffuses in the opposite direction. Some large insects squeeze their bodies to help the gases on their way.

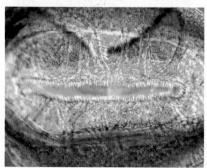

◀ AIR HOLE

Each trachea starts at an opening called a spiracle, on the side of an insect's body. This picture shows a single spiracle of a silkworm—in real life, the air hole is less than a millimeter across. Spiracles look like portholes and they have muscles that can make them open or shut. When an insect is flying, or working hard, it opens up its spiracles so that lots of oxygen can reach its muscles. When it is inactive, it keeps the spiracles almost closed.

INSIDE A BUMBLE BEE

NERVOUS SYSTEM

① **Brain:** This receives signals from sense organs and triggers muscles to move.

② **Nerve cord:** This double cord carries signals between the brain and the rest of the body.

③ **Ganglia:** These minibrains operate independently, controlling the muscles in different parts of the body.

CIRCULATORY SYSTEM

④ **Hemolymph:** Insect blood flows through body spaces, rather than through arteries and veins.

⑤ **Heart:** This muscular tube pumps blood toward the head. Valves stop the blood from flowing back.

RESPIRATORY SYSTEM

⑥ **Tracheae:** These branching tubes carry oxygen into the body and allow carbon dioxide to flow out.

DIGESTIVE SYSTEM

⑦ **Crop:** Nectar stored here is regurgitated into the nest's cells. It then ripens to become honey.

⑧ **Mid gut:** Here food is broken down into simple substances and absorbed into the body.

⑨ **Hind gut:** This part of the gut absorbs water and salts, and gets rid of the insect's waste.

DEFENSE SYSTEM

⑩ **Poison sac:** In bees and other stinging insects, this stores venom and keeps it ready for use.

⑪ **Sting:** This can inject venom into an attacker.

Each chain contains up to a dozen eggs

▲ REPRODUCTIVE SYSTEM

Clinging to a leaf, this map butterfly is laying chains of eggs. The eggs are produced by her reproductive system, which is in her abdomen. During the breeding season, female insects often look much fatter than males because their abdomens are swollen with eggs waiting to be laid. Most insects lay eggs, but not all. During spring and summer, aphids and some other sap-sucking bugs give birth to live young.

anatomy

LIVING LARDER ▶

The shape of an insect's digestive system depends on the type of food that it eats. Bloodsuckers and nectar-eaters have short intestines, but predators and seed-eaters often have a muscular pouch, called a gizzard, that grinds up their food. This honeypot ant is even more specialized—its abdomen stores nectar and swells up like a balloon. It lives in semidesert habitats, and in the drought season food is scarce. During this time, it regurgitates its nutritious fluid for other ants in the nest.

Hard abdominal plate

Abdomen swells to the size of a raisin

INSECT SENSES

If insects were as big as we are, some of their eyes would be as large as footballs and their antennae would be up to 7 ft (2 m) long. Fortunately, insects never reach this size, but their senses play a vital part in their lives. For us, sight is the most important sense, and it is for many insects too. Most insects also have a superb sense of smell, and some can hear sounds over ³/₄ mile (1 km) away. Insects use their senses to find food, track down a mate, and avoid being caught.

◄ COMPOUND EYES

Unlike vertebrates (animals with backbones), insects have compound eyes. A compound eye is split into lots of separate facets (units), each with its own lens. Each facet works like a mini-eye, collecting light from a small part of the view. Some insects have a few facets in each eye, but horse flies and dragonflies have many thousands. This gives them a detailed picture of their surroundings—although not quite as good as ours.

WHAT INSECTS SEE

HUMAN VISION
Human eyes have a single lens. The lens focuses light on a screen called a retina, like a projector at the movies. The retina is packed with millions of light-sensitive nerves. These register differences in brightness and color, sending signals to the brain. Our brains then process the signals, building up a picture of what our eyes see.

INSECT VISION
When an insect looks at the same scene, it sees it in a different way. Each facet (unit) in its eyes looks at a narrow part of the view. The signals from all the facets then travel to the insect's brain. Here, the brain adds up the signals, creating a composite picture of the outside world. Insects' vision is not as detailed as ours.

THREATENING GAZE ►
This horse fly's compound eyes cover most of its face. Unlike our eyes, its eyes cannot move, but because they bulge outward, it gets a good all-around view. As well as compound eyes, many insects have three small eyes, or ocelli, on the top of their heads. These eyes each have a single lens. They register light levels, but they do not form a picture.

Colored stripes form when light is reflected by the facets in the eye

e ►► senses

Sharp mouthparts used for cutting skin

Sucking mouthparts used for drinking bloo

NECTAR GUIDES ►
Insects see fewer colors than we do—for example, they are not nearly so sensitive to red. However, many of them can sense ultraviolet light, a color that we cannot see. Plants often use ultraviolet markings to attract insects to their flowers. These markings are called nectar guides. They steer insects toward the center of a flower, so that they can collect a meal of nectar, and carry pollen from one flower to the next.

Nectar guides show up under ultraviolet lighting

In normal daylight, the nectar guides are invisible

EARS AND ANTENNAE ►
Many insects communicate by sound, but their ears are not always on their heads. Crickets have their ears on their legs, while grasshoppers and moths have them on the sides of their abdomens. Moths use their ears as an early warning system, to listen out for flying bats. An insect's antennae (feelers) are multipurpose sense organs. They can smell, touch, and taste, and they can also pick up vibrations in the air.

Ear in recess just below knee joint

Antennae are made of a string of segments for mobility

Fine touch-sensitive hairs are scattered all over the cricket's body

SEEING MOVEMENT

HUMAN VISION
Humans have complex brains, so we are very good at analyzing what we see. A moving wasp instantly catches our attention, but we also make out still objects in the background, like the flower behind the wasp. Even if an insect keeps absolutely still, we can often spot its outline, and see that it is there.

DRAGONFLY VISION
A dragonfly has a far simpler brain, and it responds mainly to movement. Its eyes respond to the flying wasp, but they barely register the background behind it. Most predatory insects see in the same way. They can spot moving prey, but they cannot see things that keep still. To find them, they use touch or smell.

TYPES OF ANTENNAE

MOSQUITO
Antennae vary between species of insect and between males and females as well. This female mosquito has slender antennae, which she uses to track down her next meal. Male mosquitoes have bushy antennae. They use them to sense the females' wingbeats in the air, so that they can find them in the dark.

COCKCHAFER
Cockchafers have stubby antennae that can open out like a fan. The fan is made up of lots of separate plates that pick up chemicals carried by the air. Antennae like this are strong and sturdy—a good design for insects such as beetles that spend a lot of time clambering around on plants and on the ground.

EMPEROR MOTH
Male moths have some of the most sensitive antennae in the insect world. They look like feathers, and they are covered with fine filaments (strands) that sense chemicals in the air. Male moths use their antennae to pick up the scent of females. They can sense a single female several miles upwind.

INSECT BEHAVIOR

Compared to humans, insects have simple nervous systems, and their brains are often smaller than the head of a pin. Despite this, they have quick reactions, and they often behave in complex ways. All of them know how to search for food, how to escape danger, and how to track down a mate. Some can perform much more impressive feats, such as navigating their way across featureless sand or building elaborate nests. Insect behavior is controlled mainly by instinct. Instinct is like a computer program that is built into an insect's brain. It tells an insect what to do, how to do it, and often when to do it as well.

instinct

RAPID REACTIONS ▶
The instant a house fly senses danger, it takes emergency action and launches itself into the air. To do this, it relies on its fast-acting nervous system. The trigger for launch usually comes when its eyes spot movement overhead. Special nerves flash signals from the eyes to the insect's flight muscles, powering up its wings. At the same time, the fly stows away its tongue and pushes up with its legs. By now, its wings are already buzzing, and in fraction of a second, it is on its way.

Eyes sense movement above

▼ BRAINS AND MINIBRAINS
Like all insects, this cockroach has a brain in its head and a nerve cord that runs the length of its body. The nerve cord works like a data cable. It collects signals from sense organs and carries them to the brain, and it carries signals from the brain to the muscles. The nerve cord also has a series of ganglia (minibrains) that control regions of the body, so parts of the body can work on their own. However, the brain is in overall command.

0.0 SECONDS FLY SENSES MOVEMENT

Tongue is extended while the fly is feeding

Eyes are connected to brain via major nerves

Routine leg movements are controlled by ganglia

BUILT-IN CLOCKS ▲
These two cockroaches have been caught on camera, feeding after dark. Like all insects, cockroaches cannot tell the time. Instead, their activities are controlled by a chemical clock that ticks away inside their brains. This built-in clock keeps insects in step with the world around them, and it makes sure that they come out at night. If cockroaches are kept in 24-hour daylight, they still come out at night, even though it is not dark.

Wings immediately start to beat

Fly heads toward light to escape danger

**0.2 SECONDS
FLY TAKES OFF**

Tongue retracts

Legs push against ground, helping fly to take off

**0.1 SECONDS
EMERGENCY ESCAPE ACTIVATED**

Bright colors warn that the larva has an unpleasant taste

FINDING THE WAY HOME

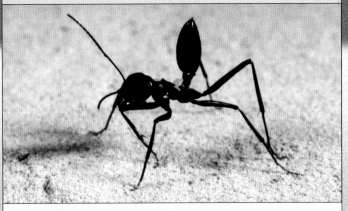

Wearing a blue identification mark, this desert ant is helping scientists to discover how insects find their way. The ant nests in sandy ground, and it travels up to 650 ft (200 m) to find food. When it leaves the nest, it follows a zigzag path. On its return, it heads back in a straight line, even when the nest is too far away to be seen.

How does the ant do this? The most likely possibility is that it uses polarized light from the sky as a compass. This shows it the fastest way back.

▲ INSECT REFLEXES

Clinging on to a potato stem, these Colorado beetle larvae look like easy targets for predatory birds. The larvae do not have wings, and their legs are small, so they cannot run away. But if anything touches them, the larvae perform a simple but effective trick—they let go of the stems with their legs and drop to the ground. Once the coast is clear, they slowly make their way back up the plant. This kind of behavior is called a reflex. It can save an insect's life, but it requires almost no brainpower at all.

▲ INSECT INTELLIGENCE

Holding a pebble in her jaws, this female sand wasp is hammering shut the entrance to her nest. It is a remarkable piece of behavior, because tool-users are practically unknown in the insect world. Once the nest is sealed up, the wasp puts the pebble back on the ground. Tool-using makes sand wasps look intelligent, but they are not quite as smart at they seem. When a sand wasp picks up a pebble, it is simply following its instincts. Unlike a human or a chimp, it does not understand how tools work.

INSECTS ON THE MOVE

With a kick of its powerful back legs, a locust can throw itself about 7 ft (2 m) through the air. It is an impressive feat, and also a very practical way of escaping attack. Many other insects jump, but even more use all six legs at once to scuttle their way across the ground. Compared to humans, insects weigh very little, and this affects the way they move. They can stop and start almost instantly, and they find it almost as easy to run uphill as down. Their small size also has another benefit—if they fall or land badly, they hardly ever get hurt.

MOVING WITHOUT LEGS

Many insect larvae move by wriggling because they do not have any legs. This wormlike animal is the larva of a flea. Unlike adult fleas, it lives among discarded fur and feathers and feeds on specks of dried blood and pieces of skin. Other legless larvae bore through their food. They include maggots (the larvae of flies) and also the larvae of wood-boring beetles and sawflies. For these young insects, not having legs is an advantage, because they would get in the way.

MUSCLES AT WORK ▶
This diagram shows the muscles that power a locust's legs. A locust's muscles are inside its legs, and they work by pulling on its exoskeleton. They normally work in pairs: here, the muscle colored blue bends the leg joint, while the one colored red straightens it out. An insect's muscles work best in warm conditions. When it is hot, insects can move very quickly. When it is cold, they sometimes come to a complete halt.

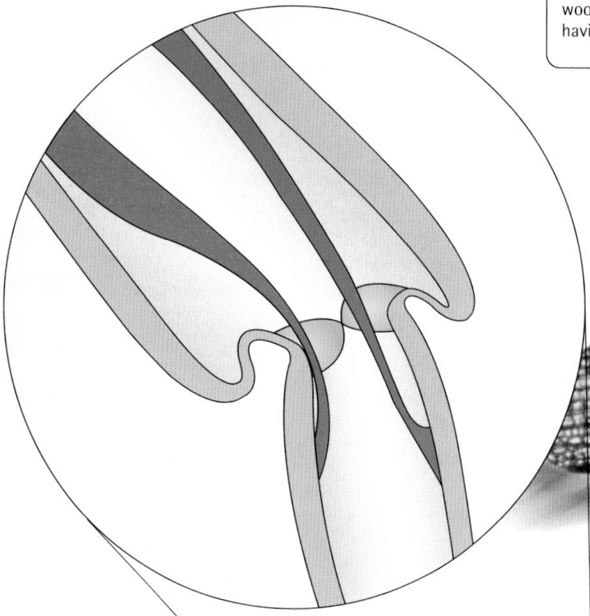

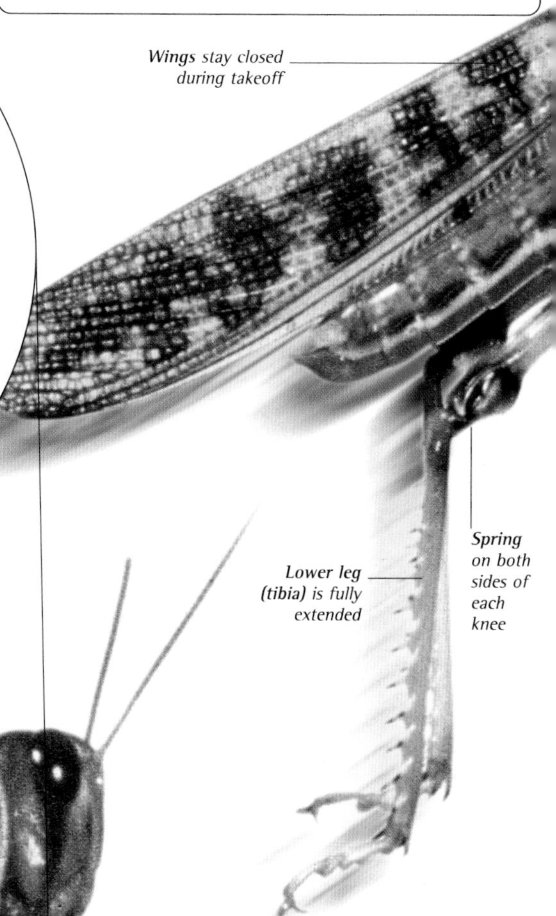

Wings stay closed during takeoff

Knee fully bent to position feet toward front of body

Wings folded over back

Lower leg (tibia) is fully extended

Spring on both sides of each knee

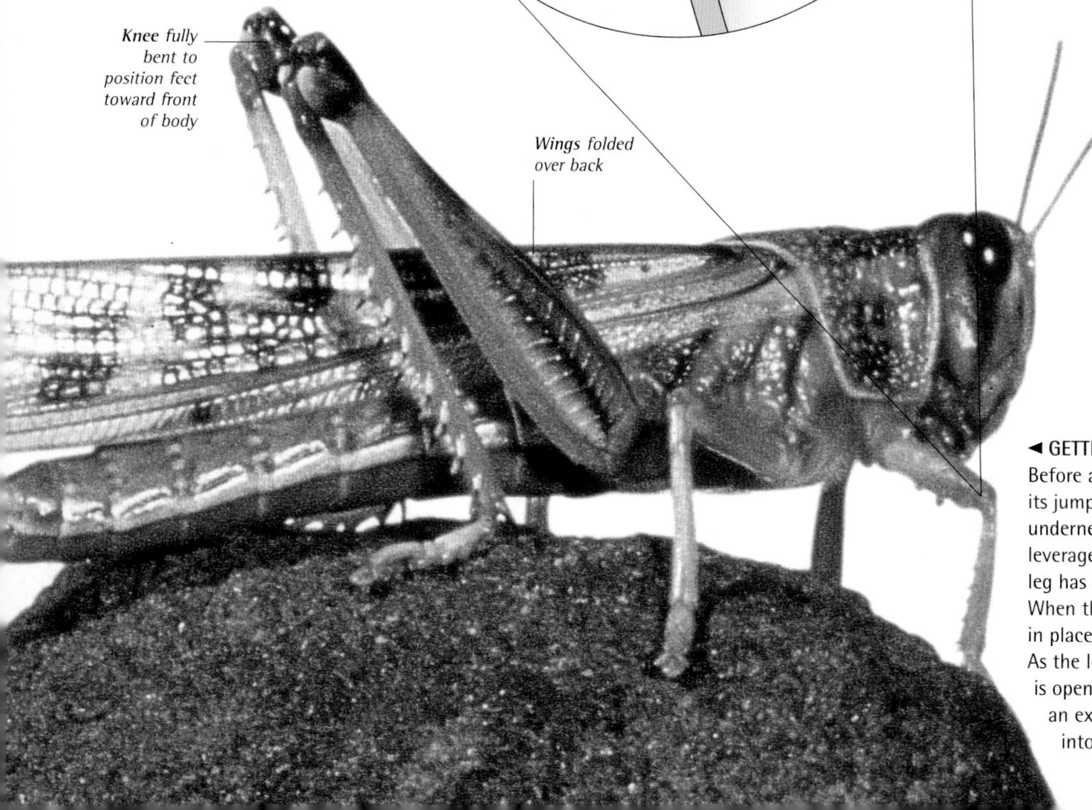

◀ GETTING READY TO JUMP
Before a locust takes off, it is already preparing for its jump. It folds up its hind legs, and tucks its feet underneath its body. This gives its legs maximum leverage when they straighten out. The locust's hind leg has a spring in its knee and stretchy tendons. When the hind legs are folded back they are held in place by a special catch inside the knee joint. As the leg muscles contract, the catch in the knee is opened, and the leg suddenly straightens with an explosive kick, launching the locust into the air.

23

▼ LIFTOFF

When the locust jumps, its hind legs straighten out, and it folds its other legs backward to make itself more streamlined. Once the locust is in the air, it either opens its wings and flies away or drops back to the ground. The hind legs remain streamlined, but the front legs stretch out as the locust lands again. A big jump can cover over 40 times the locust's length.

Short antennae

Biting jaws for feeding on plants

Front legs swing backward

movement

INSECT LEGS

WATER BOATMAN

Like many freshwater insects, the water boatman uses its legs as oars. It hind legs are specially adapted for this work, with a flat shape and a fringe of hairs that helps them to push against the water. Legs like these do not work well out of water, so instead of walking from pond to pond, water boatmen fly.

MOLE CRICKET

With its spade-shaped front legs and armored head, the mole cricket is built like a tunneling machine. It spends most of its life underground, pushing through the soil and feeding mainly on plant roots. Unlike other crickets, it does not have powerful back legs. It can crawl and fly, but it cannot jump.

STICK INSECT

A stick insect's legs are long and spindly, and its feet have hooked claws to give it a good grip. Stick insects rely on their camouflaged exoskeleton for protection, and their legs play a part too. When a stick insect moves, it often sways from side to side. This makes it look like part of a plant, moving gently in the wind.

TIGER BEETLE
8 FT/SEC (2.5 M/SEC)

COCKROACH
5 FT/SEC (1.5 M/SEC)

FIELD CRICKET
6 IN/SEC (0.15 M/SEC)

ARMY ANT
2 IN/SEC (0.05 M/SEC)

◄ INSECT ATHLETES

Insect speeds are difficult to measure, because insects rarely run for long. However, the title of fastest-running insect almost certainly goes to predatory tiger beetles—they can sprint at 8 ft/sec (2.5 m/sec), which is the same as a gentle jog. Cockroaches are not quite so fast, but they are extremely quick off the mark. At the other end of the scale, army ants cover only 2 in/sec (5 cm/sec). However, even at this speed, their swarms can overtake many insects in their path.

Body loops as prolegs move close to front legs

Body stretches out

Prolegs release grip prior to back end moving forwards

Front (true) legs grip tightly

▲ WALKING IN A LOOP

Caterpillars have six true legs at the front of their bodies and several pairs of suckerlike prolegs at the rear. In this looper caterpillar, or inchworm, the two kinds of legs are set far apart, allowing the caterpillar to move in an unusual way. First, it gets a good grip with its prolegs, and reaches forward as far as it can. It then releases its prolegs and pulls its body forward in a loop.

Prolegs anchor themselves after moving forward

Prolegs grip tightly

Head moves forward

BEETLES

If you pick an insect at random, there is a good chance that it will be a beetle. That is because beetles are the most successful insects on Earth. So far, scientists have identified nearly 400,000 different species—some are only just visible to the naked eye, while others are as big as an adult's hand. Adult beetles have extra-tough bodies and strong legs, but their most important feature is their hardened forewings, which fit over their hindwings like a case. With this special protection, they can clamber around in all kinds of places to search for food.

beetles

BEETLES ORDER

Beetles make up the order Coleoptera—the largest order of insects, containing about 37 percent of all the known species in the insect world. Beetles live in all land habitats, and they are also found in freshwater. Many beetles—particularly hunters and scavengers—come out to feed at night.

Small, hooked feet give beetle firm grip

GENTLE GIANT ▶

Weighing up to 4 oz (100 g)—about three times as much as a mouse—Goliath beetles are the heaviest insects in the world. Like most beetles, these tropical monsters have hardened forewings, called elytra, which protect the more delicate hind wings. When a beetle flies, the elytra open up, but only the hind wings beat. Goliath beetles feed on forest flowers and have small heads with stubby mouthparts. They have strong legs that end in hooked feet.

Elytra meet in a line down the middle of the beetle's back

Filmy hind wings are stowed away beneath the elytra

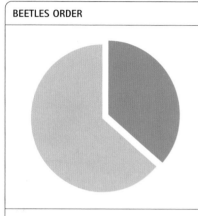

◀ BEETLE COLORS

Many beetles are jet black, but some have eye-catching colors. This tropical leaf beetle, from Southeast Asia, is iridescent, with a beautiful metallic sheen. Some scarab beetles glisten like pieces of gold, while many smaller beetles have bright stripes or spots, warning predators that they are dangerous to eat. Wasp beetles have a bold yellow and black pattern—a color scheme that makes other animals think they can sting.

Surface markings vary from beetle to beetle like a fingerprint

Shield covering
front of beetle's head

Flattened legs
with defensive
spines

Compound
eyes

Antennae are
small and
club-shaped

Silky hairs
on legs

▲ PREDATORY BEETLE

Like many beetles, ladybugs hunt living prey. They feed on aphids and mites, eating dozens of them a day. A ladybug's jaws are small but sharp, and they turn food into a sticky pulp. Aphids move quite slowly, so ladybugs find it easy to catch them. Other predatory beetles include ground beetles. These hunt faster prey and need to be quicker. They are some of the swiftest runners in the insect world, reaching speeds of up to 6 mph (9 km/h).

▲ SCAVENGING BEETLE

The churchyard beetle is a typical scavenger, coming out to feed after dark. It lives on the dead remains of animals and plants, and also on any small live animals that come its way. Scavenging beetles clear up all kinds of natural waste, which helps to break down nutrients so they can be used by plants again and again. These beetles can cause problems if they get indoors, because some of them eat stored food.

Long snout
reaches deep into food

Body camouflaged
by short hairs

PLANT-EATING BEETLE ▶

With its long snout tipped by tiny jaws, this weevil chews its way into nuts. It is one of thousands of different beetles that live on plant food. Some beetles attack plants from the outside, but many beetle grubs bore their way in, so that they are surrounded by their food. Plant-feeding beetles are not always bad for plants. Many of them visit flowers, and as they feed they spread pollen, helping plants to make seeds.

LADYBUG STAGES OF DEVELOPMENT

EGGS
Beetles develop by complete metamorphosis, which means that they change shape completely as they grow up. Like most insects, they start life as eggs. This batch of ladybug eggs is a few days old. The young grubs, or larvae, are just visible through the eggs' shells and will soon be ready to hatch.

HATCHING
When a beetle larva hatches, its first meal is often the shell of its own egg. At this stage, the larva is tiny, but it soon starts to feed and grow. Beetle larvae are very varied. Ladybug larvae have strong jaws and stubby legs, but weevil larvae are usually legless. They move by burrowing through their food.

GROWING UP
At two weeks old, a ladybug larva has a big appetite and spends most of its time eating. At this stage, it still looks nothing like its parents. Once it has molted its skin several times, the larva stops feeding and turns into a pupa. Inside the pupa, its body is broken down and an adult one is assembled in its place.

ADULTHOOD
When its body is fully formed, the adult ladybug breaks out of its pupal case. Like most adult beetles, it has working wings. If food is short, it can fly away to find somewhere new to feed and breed. Compared to other insects, adult beetles are generally long-lived. Adult ladybugs can live for over a year.

WINGS

Insects were the first animals to have flapping wings. Although their wings are small, they are amazingly effective, and there are few places on land that flying insects cannot reach. Most insects have four wings, although true flies have only two. Their wings are usually thin and transparent, but in some insects—such as beetles—the forewings are thickened for extra strength. Once an insect's wings have developed, they cannot grow any more. If the wings are damaged in any way, they cannot be repaired.

flight

*Elytra fit tightly
over the abdomen*

*Male
cockchafer's
antennae
open out
like a fan*

*Elytra hinge upward and outward as
the cockchafer prepares for takeoff*

▼ TAKEOFF

Flies can take off almost instantly, but for this cockchafer beetle, getting airborne takes more time. Like most beetles, cockchafers have two very different pairs of wings. Their forewings, or elytra, are as stiff as plastic and they fit over the hind wings like a case. Before it can take off, the cockchafer first has to open its elytra and swing them apart. Once it has done this, it can unfold its hind wings and launch itself into the air.

*Elytra do not flap
during flight*

*Surface of abdomen
usually covered by wings*

*Pointed abdomen
juts out when
wings are closed*

*Hind wings
unfold to their
full length*

INSECT WING TYPES

AZURE DAMSELFLY
A damselfly has two almost identical pairs of wings. Both pairs are long and slender and fold backward over the damselfly's body when it is at rest. Damselflies are not fast fliers, but their wings can beat in different directions at once. This means that they can hover on the spot, or reverse in midair.

HOUSE FLY
House flies have just one pair of streamlined wings. Their wings are much shorter than a damselfly's wings, but they beat much faster, making the fly speed through the air. The wings fold back when the fly lands, but they can open out very quickly— the perfect thing for an emergency getaway.

COMMON WASP
Wasps have two pairs of filmy wings. The forewings are much longer than the hind wings, but when the wasp flies, they beat together because they are joined by a row of tiny hooks. Wasp wings look narrow when they are folded. To protect them, hibernating wasps sometimes tuck them under their legs.

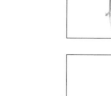

PLUME MOTH
Moths and butterflies have two pairs of wings that are covered in microscopic scales. Their wings are usually broad and flat, but a plume moth's are divided into feathery tufts. When a plume moth lands, the tufts fold up like a fan, but the wings stick out from the body, making a shape like the letter T.

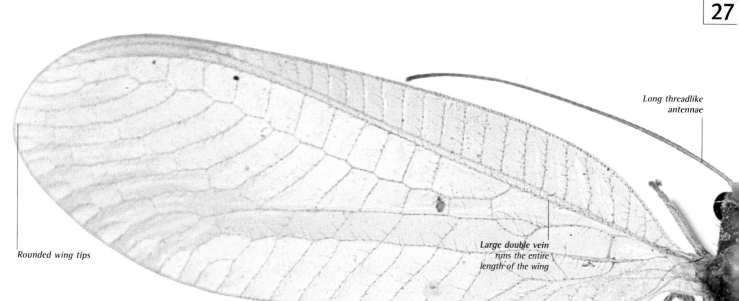

Long threadlike antennae

Rounded wing tips

Large double vein runs the entire length of the wing

WING STRUTS ►

With its wings spread out wide, it is easy to see how a lacewing gets its name. Like all insects, its wings are crisscrossed by a network of narrow veins. The veins work like struts, strengthening the wings as they beat up and down. When insects start adult life, their wings are crumpled and soft. Blood starts to flow through the veins, making the wings open out. After several hours, the wings dry out, making them stiff enough to fly.

Wing attached to muscles inside thorax

Hind wings beat independently of forewings

Small cross-veins divide the wing into separate panels

Male vaporer moth

Female vaporer moth

DISPOSABLE WINGS

Wings are very useful, but they can get in the way. Some insects avoid this problem by shedding their wings once they no longer need them. This parasitic deer fly has shed its wings after landing on a deer. It feeds on blood and will spend the rest of its life scuttling through the deer's fur.

Other wing-shedders include flying ants and flying termites. They do not fly far—usually only to establish a new nest with a new queen. They often bite off their wings when they reach the site of the new nest. Without wings, it is much easier for them to start building the nest.

▲ WINGLESS INSECTS

The world's most primitive insects, such as bristletails, never have wings. Many other insects have lost the ability to fly over thousands of years. They even include some butterflies and moths. This picture shows a male and female vaporer moth. The male has wings, but the female does not. She looks like a fat furry grub and can only crawl. The female never moves from her pupa: after mating, she lays eggs and dies there. The male needs his wings to locate the females.

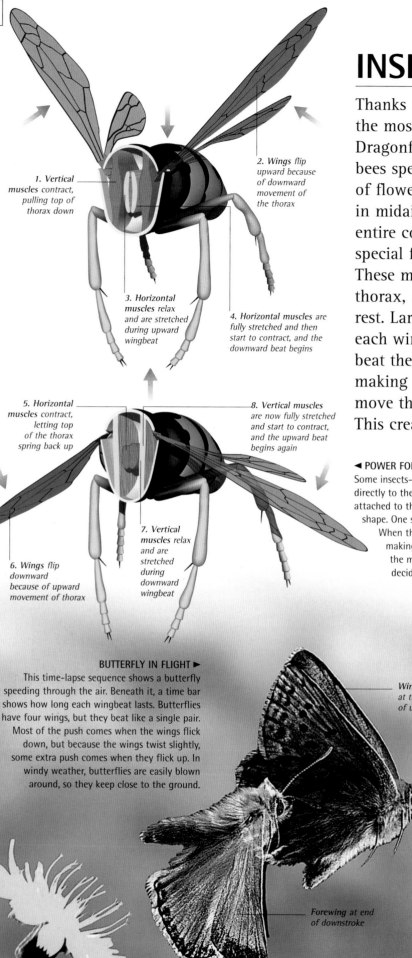

1. *Vertical muscles* contract, pulling top of thorax down

2. *Wings flip upward because of downward movement of the thorax*

3. *Horizontal muscles* relax and are stretched during upward wingbeat

4. *Horizontal muscles* are fully stretched and then start to contract, and the downward beat begins

5. *Horizontal muscles* contract, letting top of the thorax spring back up

8. *Vertical muscles* are now fully stretched and start to contract, and the upward beat begins again

7. *Vertical muscles* relax and are stretched during downward wingbeat

6. *Wings flip downward because of upward movement of thorax*

INSECT FLIGHT

Thanks to their small size, insects are some of the most impressive fliers in the animal world. Dragonflies dart through the air after prey, and bees speed over fields and gardens in search of flowers. Hover flies can stay rock-steady in midair, while butterflies can migrate across entire continents. To do all this, insects use special flight muscles that power their wings. These muscles are packed inside an insect's thorax, and they can work for hours without a rest. Large butterflies flap their wings slowly, so each wingbeat is easy to see. But many insects beat their wings hundreds of times a second, making them vanish in a blur. When wings move this quickly, they make the air vibrate. This creates a buzzing or whining sound.

◄ POWER FOR FLIGHT
Some insects—including dragonflies—have flight muscles that are attached directly to the wings. But in more advanced fliers, such as wasps, they are attached to the thorax. These muscles work by making the thorax change shape. One set pulls vertically, making the top of the thorax move down. When this happens, the wings flick up. Another set pulls horizontally, making the wings drop back down. Once the wings start beating, the muscles continue to work automatically until the insect decides to land.

BUTTERFLY IN FLIGHT ►
This time-lapse sequence shows a butterfly speeding through the air. Beneath it, a time bar shows how long each wingbeat lasts. Butterflies have four wings, but they beat like a single pair. Most of the push comes when the wings flick down, but because the wings twist slightly, some extra push comes when they flick up. In windy weather, butterflies are easily blown around, so they keep close to the ground.

Wings separate again, lowering air pressure above butterfly

Wings touch at the end of upstroke

Downstroke pushes butterfly upward and forward

Forewing at end of downstroke

0 SECONDS   0.3 SECONDS   0.5 SECONDS   0.7 SECONDS

◄ WARMING UP

Insect flight muscles work best when they are warm. When the temperature drops below about 50°F (10°C), many insects are too cold to take off. But not all insects are like this. Bumble bees shiver to warm up their muscles—after a few minutes their flight muscles can be 68°F (20°C) warmer than the air outside. This Arctic bumble bee is feeding on flowers in Greenland, which is less than 465 miles (750 km) from the chilly North Pole.

FRUIT FLY
0.1 MPH (0.2 KM/H)

HONEY BEE
14 MPH (22 KM/H)

DESERT LOCUST
20 MPH (33 KM/H)

DEATH'S HEAD HAWK MOTH
33 MPH (54 KM/H)

DRAGONFLY
35 MPH (58 KM/H)

flight

UNDERCARRIAGE ►

Many flying insects use their legs to launch themselves into the air. This scorpion fly has taken off with a helpful kick. Scorpion flies are very weak fliers, so they choose a high point from which to jump. Crickets and grasshoppers give a bigger push—once they are airborne, they can open their wings and fly away. During flight some insects fold their legs away, but many spread them out. This helps them to balance, and also makes it easier to land.

▲ FLIGHT SPEEDS

Insects often fly in short bursts, which makes it difficult to measure their speeds. Many cruise slowly, but speed up if they are in danger, or if they are chasing their prey. This chart shows flight speeds for a range of different insects. At 35 mph (58 km/h), dragonflies can overtake most other insects, and even some small birds. However, they cannot keep flying at top speed for long, because their bodies begin to overheat.

Wings reach end of next upstroke

Single surface created by forewing and hind wing

Wings move toward end of downstroke

Edges flex as the wings move down

1 SECOND   1.3 SECONDS   1.5 SECONDS   1.7 SECONDS   2 SECONDS

DRAGONFLIES AND DAMSELFLIES

Speeding over fields and ponds, dragonflies are some of the fastest-flying hunters in the insect world. They feed on other insects, overtaking their prey and then grabbing them in midair. There are about 5,500 species of dragonflies and damselflies, and all of them have large eyes, long bodies, and two pairs of transparent wings. Dragonflies usually rest with their wings held out, but damselflies fold theirs along their backs. Young dragonflies and damselflies live in freshwater and take up to three years to grow up. During their underwater development, they feed on other animals, catching them with a lightning-fast stab of their jaws.

dragonflies

DRAGONFLIES AND DAMSELFLIES ORDER

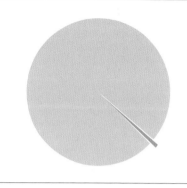

The order Odonata makes up 0.5 percent of all the world's insects species. Most dragonflies and damselflies live close to freshwater or in damp habitats. Dragonflies are usually larger than damselflies, but rain forest damselflies have the longest wings—7 in (19 cm) from tip to tip.

Enormous eyes cover most of the head

Forewings and *hind wings* are similar size

Powerful jaws crunch up food

Deep thorax packed with flight muscles

Legs can be held out like a basket to catch prey

▲ MIDAIR KILLER

With its strong wings and sturdy legs, this dragonfly is superbly equipped for ambushing and catching its prey. Inside its extra-large thorax are powerful flight muscles that beat its wings. Unlike most insects, a dragonfly's wings beat in opposite directions, enabling it to fly backward or hover on the spot. Dragonflies have very long abdomens and people often imagine that they can sting; however, they cannot. Instead, dragonflies and damselflies kill their prey with their powerful legs and jaws.

EMPEROR DRAGONFLY DEVELOPMENT

EGGS
Dragonflies and damselflies develop by incomplete metamorphosis, which means that they change shape gradually as they grow. The adults lay their eggs in water. Many dragonflies simply drop them onto the surface of the water, but damselflies often climb into the water itself.

YOUNG NYMPH
Young dragonflies and damselflies are known as nymphs. When they hatch, they have well-developed legs and eyes and sharp stabbing jaws. They breathe through a set of gills. Nymphs are often well camouflaged. They lurk on the bottom of streams and ponds, attacking any small animals that come within range.

MATURE NYMPH
During its life underwater, the nymph sheds its skin several times. After each molt, it gets bigger and its wing buds become more developed. Finally, in spring or summer, the nymph climbs out of the water and molts for a final time. Its outer skin splits open, and an adult dragonfly slowly pulls itself free.

ADULT
Adult dragonflies have working wings. Their eyes are larger than the nymphs' and are designed for working in air. The adults are also more colorful. Many have bright metallic bands on their abdomens, and some have smoky patches on their wings. The markings often vary between males and females, making it easy to tell them apart.

▲ HUNTING UNDERWATER
This dragonfly larva has caught a stickleback fish. It hunts by stealth, ambushing or stalking its prey. When it is close enough, it shoots out a set of hinged mouthparts, known as a mask. The mask is tipped with two spiky claws and works like a harpoon, stabbing and then pulling in the prey. Young damselflies are less powerful and eat smaller water animals.

▲ HUNTING IN THE AIR
Adult dragonflies usually spot their prey by patrolling through the air. This dragonfly has just caught a meal and has settled down to feed. It uses its feet to catch its prey and also to hold it down as it starts to eat. Damselflies use a different technique—they either sit and wait for insects to fly past or snatch them from waterside plants.

Transparent wings with prominent veins

PAIRING UP ▶
Dragonflies and damselflies have a unique way of mating—these two damselflies show how it is done. The male, on the left, grips the female behind the head, using a pair of special claspers on his tail. Meanwhile, the female's tail reaches forward to touch the male, so that her eggs can be fertilized. The mating pair can fly like this, and they often stay paired up while the female lays her eggs.

Male clasps female behind her head

Female's abdomen collects sperm from the male

Long, sticklike abdomen for a streamlined shape

PREDATORY INSECTS

Insects have many enemies, but the most deadly are often other insects. Some chase their prey in the open, while others use stealth, taking their victims by surprise. Some do not feed until their prey is dead, but praying mantises start right away, while their meal is still struggling to escape. Predatory insects eat a huge range of small animals, including other insects, spiders, mites, fish, and frogs. Some of these are troublesome pests, so predatory insects can help to keep them under control.

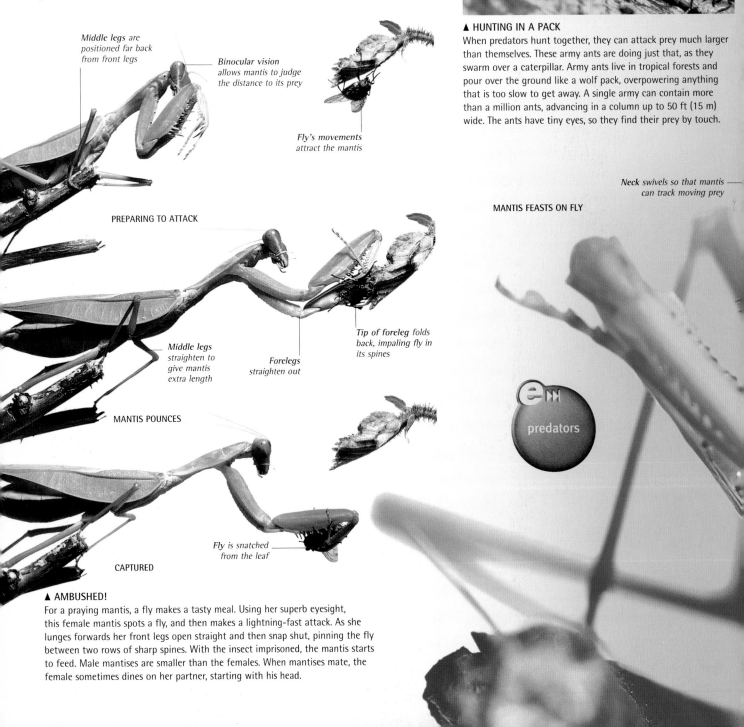

▲ HUNTING IN A PACK
When predators hunt together, they can attack prey much larger than themselves. These army ants are doing just that, as they swarm over a caterpillar. Army ants live in tropical forests and pour over the ground like a wolf pack, overpowering anything that is too slow to get away. A single army can contain more than a million ants, advancing in a column up to 50 ft (15 m) wide. The ants have tiny eyes, so they find their prey by touch.

Middle legs are positioned far back from front legs

Binocular vision allows mantis to judge the distance to its prey

Fly's movements attract the mantis

PREPARING TO ATTACK

Neck swivels so that mantis can track moving prey

MANTIS FEASTS ON FLY

Middle legs straighten to give mantis extra length

Forelegs straighten out

Tip of foreleg folds back, impaling fly in its spines

MANTIS POUNCES

predators

Fly is snatched from the leaf

CAPTURED

▲ AMBUSHED!
For a praying mantis, a fly makes a tasty meal. Using her superb eyesight, this female mantis spots a fly, and then makes a lightning-fast attack. As she lunges forwards her front legs open straight and then snap shut, pinning the fly between two rows of sharp spines. With the insect imprisoned, the mantis starts to feed. Male mantises are smaller than the females. When mantises mate, the female sometimes dines on her partner, starting with his head.

Threadlike antennae

WASP STING ▶
To make a kill, predatory insects have to overpower their victims. Many use their legs or mouthparts to grab their prey, but wasps often follow this up with a deadly sting. The sting slides out of the wasp's abdomen, and a muscular pouch pumps venom through the sting and into the victim's body. Unlike wasps, bees are not predatory. Their stings often have barbed tips, but they use them only in self-defense.

Venom sac

Muscular pouch

Large, forward-facing eyes

Hollow sting housed in abdomen

Small, but powerful jaws bite into the fly's body

Spines press in from both sides to grip prey

▲ LIVING LARDERS
Some insects hunt on behalf of their young. This wasp has caught a spider and has paralyzed it with her sting. She will drag the spider back to an underground nest, where it will be a living food store for one of her grubs. There are many species of hunting wasps, and they specialize in different types of prey, from caterpillars to tarantulas. Only the females hunt—the males usually feed on flowers.

DEALING WITH A MEAL

This glow-worm larva has attacked a snail and is starting to feed. The larva stabs the snail with its jaws, and then dribbles digestive fluids into its body. The snail dissolves into a nutritious soup, and the larva sucks up its food.

Other predators also use this method of attack. Some lacewing larvae use their prey as camouflage as well. Once they have sucked up their victims, they attach the empty skins to their backs—a gruesome but effective way of hiding.

SKATERS AND SWIMMERS

In the calm water of ponds, deadly predators are on the move. Diving beetles scud through the shallows, grabbing small fish and insects with their sharp claws. Water boatmen hang just beneath the surface, waiting to stab flying insects that crash-land. On the surface itself, pond skaters wait for their victims, feeling for tiny ripples that pinpoint struggling prey. About one in 20 insect species live in watery surroundings such as ponds, lakes, rivers, and streams. Some spend their whole lives in freshwater, while others grow up in it and then fly away.

◄ SURFACE TENSION
Instead of floating, pond skaters use surface tension to walk on water. Surface tension is a force that pulls water molecules together. When the water is calm, it makes the surface behave like a thin sheet. Pond skaters have light bodies and water-repellent feet, so they can stand on the surface without sinking through it. This photograph, taken under a special light, shows how the water makes dimples around a pond skater's feet.

Snorkel has water-repellent tip to prevent it from flooding

freshwater insects

▲ POND SKATER
Seen from the side, this pond skater shows its piercing mouthparts and long slender legs. Pond skaters eat insects that have become stranded on the surface. They use their front legs to grip their food, their middle legs to swim, and their back legs to steer. Pond skaters are true bugs, and most of them have well-developed wings. They can fly, so it is easy for them to spread from pond to pond.

◄ WATER SCORPION
Although they live in water, most freshwater insects breathe air. The water scorpion gets its air supplies through a long snorkel, which it pushes up through the surface. The snorkel passes air to its tracheal system, which delivers oxygen throughout its body. Water scorpions are carnivorous bugs, and they stalk small fish and insects in muddy water. Their weapons are stealth, good camouflage, and two strong front legs that grip and spear their prey.

◄ MAYFLY NYMPH
Mayfly nymphs that live in running water have flattened bodies and strong legs—features that prevent them from being washed away. Instead of breathing air from the surface, they collect oxygen through two rows of feathery gills. The nymphs spend up to three years underwater, preparing for an adult life that lasts less than a day.

Streamlined body with glossy surface

Flat body with mud-color camouflage

Powerful front legs for seizing prey

GREAT DIVING BEETLE ▲
With bodies up to 2 in (5 cm) long, diving beetles are powerful freshwater hunters. They swim with their back legs, speeding through the water. Before each dive, they store air under their wing cases, and they have to kick hard to stop themselves from bobbing up to the surface. Diving beetle larvae are even more aggressive than their parents, with powerful jaws that can kill tadpoles and small fish.

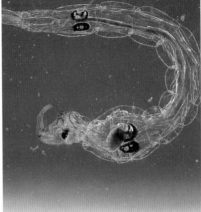

▲ SAUCER BUG

like most freshwater bugs, saucer bugs are
hunters, and they grip their victims with their
front legs, which can snap shut like a pair of
penknives. Saucer bugs lurk on the bottom of
ponds, and their camouflage helps them to
hunt. They surface to breathe, but afterward
they quickly dive back to the bottom, to hide
among plants or in the mud.

▲ WHIRLIGIG BEETLES

Predatory insects often lie in wait, but whirligig beetles are
always on the move. Like tiny black boats, they spin around on
the surface, watching for small insects that have fallen in. A
whirligig's eyes are divided into two parts. One part looks above
the surface, while the other part looks at the water underneath.
This all-around view means that whirligigs can dive after food,
and spot danger from above and below. Adult whirligigs spend
the winter buried in mud at the bottom of ponds.

▲ PHANTOM MIDGE LARVA

With its transparent body, the phantom midge
larva is an almost invisible hunter. It hangs
motionless in water and snags small animals
with its hook-shaped antennae. To change its
depth, it adjusts two pairs of onboard buoyancy
tanks, which make it rise and fall like a
submarine. In summer, the adults often gather
in dense swarms that look like clouds of smoke.

Rear legs *have
fringes for pushing
against the water*

Hind legs *are long
with an oarlike blade*

Film of air *gives the
backswimmer a silvery color*

▲ BACKSWIMMER

Hanging beneath the water's
surface, the backswimmer spends its entire life upside
down. Like pond skaters, it eats insects that have crash-
landed, but it attacks them from below. Its extra-long
hind legs work like a pair of oars, and it uses them to
swim towards its prey. Backswimmers have big eyes, and
they always keep their fronts toward the light. If they
are put in a tank that is lit from the bottom, they swim
the right way up.

Elytra *store air
underneath for
when beetle dives*

*Dragonfly eggs on
underwater plants*

▼ DRAGONFLY NYMPH

Young dragonflies—known as
nymphs—rely on stealth to hunt.
They crawl along the bottom of
ponds and lakes and up water plants,
watching for prey. If a tadpole or
small fish wanders near, they spear
it with their telescopic jaws. The
nymphs breathe by sucking water
in and out of their abdomens. If
danger threatens, they squeeze
water out of their abdomens
like jet engines—the perfect
high-speed getaway.

**Claw-tipped
front legs** *for
gripping prey*

Mouthparts—
*known as the
mask—are folded
under the head
when not in use*

Small head
with large eyes

TRICKS AND TRAPS

In the world of insects, things are not always what they seem. In caves, twinkling lights lure insects toward a sticky death. Among plants and flowers, stabbing arms and lethal jaws can strike at any time. Even the ground is not safe. Hidden beneath the surface, specialized hunters wait for the chance to make the kill. In all these places, the danger comes from insects that use trickery to catch their prey. For a predator, this kind of lifestyle makes good sense. Instead of using energy to chase its food, it waits patiently for prey to come its way.

▲ LIGHTS IN THE DARK
In Waitamo Caves in New Zealand, the darkness is broken by thousands of tiny lights. The lights are produced by gnat larvae known as glow worms. Each glow worm lowers itself into the air on slender threads of silk and switches on its light to attract flying insects. When an insect flies into the threads, it gets stuck. As it struggles to escape, the glow worm starts to feed.

e▶▶
predators

▲ DEADLY SNARES
Close up, glow worm threads look like necklaces hanging from the roof of a cave. The threads are about 2 in (5 cm) long, with "beads" that are blobs of glue. Each larva spins several threads to increase its chances of making a catch. Glow worms hunt in other dimly lit places, such as the hollowed out stumps of trees.

Petal-like flaps disguise the mantis's legs

▲ LURKING IN FLOWERS
This flower mantis has climbed into an orchid bloom and is waiting for unsuspecting insects to come its way. Flower mantises are often brightly colored with flaps that resemble a flower's petals. Flowers are good places for hunting because they have a steady stream of insect visitors. Mantises have amazingly quick reactions—sometimes they grab insects while they are still in the air.

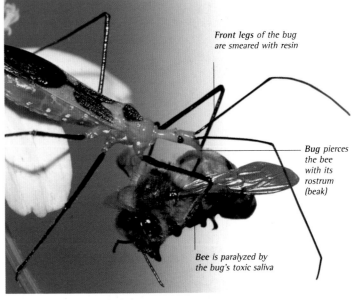

Front legs of the bug are smeared with resin

Bug pierces the bee with its rostrum (beak)

Bee is paralyzed by the bug's toxic saliva

▲ FATAL SCENT
Leaning out of a flower, this assassin bug is feeding on a bee. Assassin bugs can lure bees to their death—they smear their front legs with sticky resin, which they collect from trees. Bees like the scent of the resin, and they try to track it down. When a bee comes within range, the assassin bug attacks. The sticky resin makes it very difficult for the bee to escape.

◄ TROJAN HORSES

These caterpillars from Australia are being tended by a group of ants. The ants protect the caterpillars in their nest until the caterpillars are ready to pupate. In return, the caterpillars supply the ants with droplets of sugary food. But not all caterpillars are quite so well behaved. Some caterpillar species trick their way into ants' nests and then start feeding on their eggs and young. They mimic ant scents, which persuade worker ants to carry them to their underground nests. Amazingly, the ants cannot recognize the intruders in their midst.

ANTLION TRAPS

DEADLY JAWS
Ant lions are carnivorous insects with short legs and extra-large jaws. Some of them hunt on the ground or under stones, but most of them are too cumbersome to catch moving prey. Instead, the larvae dig special traps in loose sandy soil. Once the trap is ready, they wait for prey to come their way.

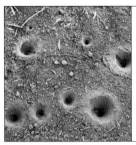

PITTED GROUND
This overhead view shows ant lion traps scattered over the ground. The traps are steep-sided pits, up to 2 in (5 cm) across. Each ant lion larva waits patiently at the bottom of its pit, with only its jaws exposed. To work, the pits have to stay dry. These traps are underneath a tree, where they are sheltered from the rain.

HOW THE TRAP WORKS
If an insect walks near the edge of the ant lion pit, it sometimes falls straight in. More often, the ant lion senses the movement and flicks it with sand. The insect is knocked off balance and starts slipping over the edge. As soon as it hits the bottom, the ant lion grabs it with its jaws and enjoys a tasty meal.

Surface of termites' nest

Antennae camouflaged with carton from the nest

Bug is almost invisible as it walks over the nest

Worker termite used as bait

DEADLY BAIT ►

Crouched over a termites' nest, this young assassin bug is fishing for its next meal. For bait, it uses a freshly killed termite, which it holds firmly in its jaws. When other termites come out to investigate, the bug kills and eats them one by one. For protection, the bug's body is camouflaged with pieces of carton—the cardboardlike material that some termites use to make their nests.

FEEDING ON BLOOD

For many insects, blood is the perfect food. It is packed with protein, which is what female insects need to make eggs. In a few minutes, a bloodsucking insect can drink enough blood to last it for several days—or even for the whole of its adult life. Bloodsucking insects live and feed in two ways. Some are temporary visitors that land, feed, and go. These include mosquitoes and many flies, as well as bugs and vampire moths. Others are parasites that live aboard their hosts full-time.

bloodsuckers

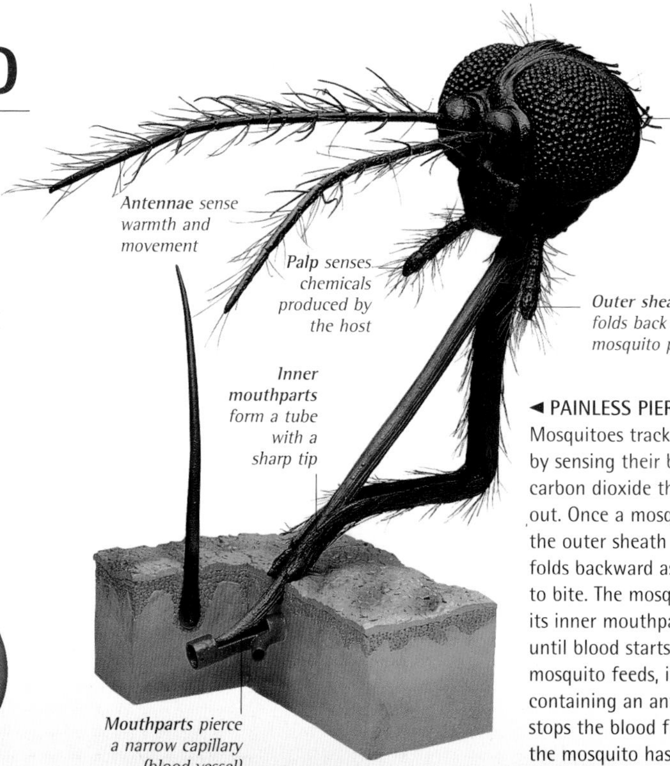

Large eye
works well even in dim light

Antennae sense warmth and movement

Palp senses chemicals produced by the host

Inner mouthparts form a tube with a sharp tip

Outer sheath
folds back as the mosquito pierces skin

◀ PAINLESS PIERCING

Mosquitoes track down their hosts by sensing their body heat and the carbon dioxide that they breathe out. Once a mosquito has landed, the outer sheath of its mouthparts folds backward as the insect begins to bite. The mosquito gently pushes its inner mouthparts into the skin until blood starts to flow. As the mosquito feeds, it injects saliva containing an anticoagulant. This stops the blood from clotting, so the mosquito has plenty of time to finish its meal.

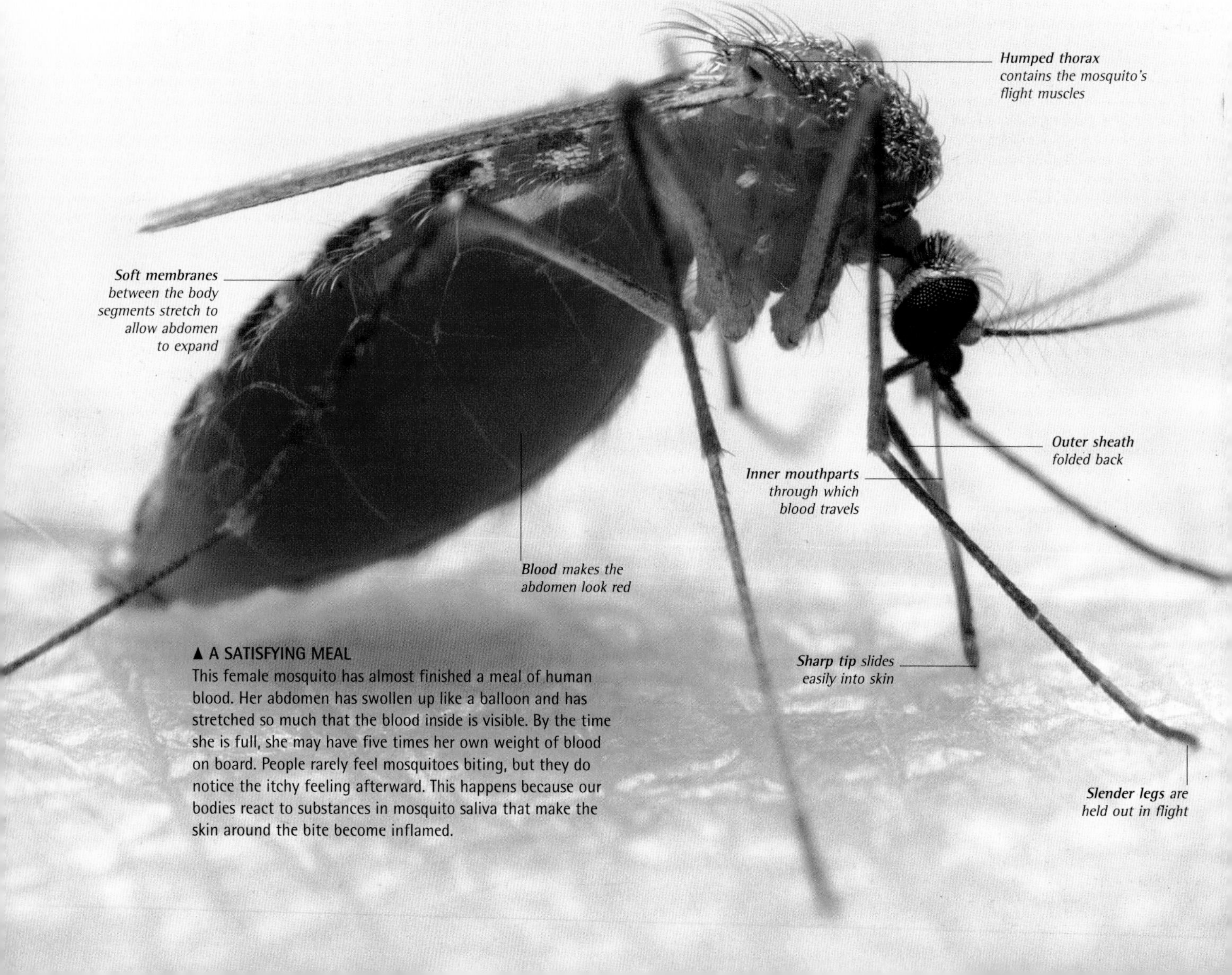

Mouthparts pierce a narrow capillary (blood vessel)

Humped thorax
contains the mosquito's flight muscles

Soft membranes between the body segments stretch to allow abdomen to expand

Outer sheath
folded back

Inner mouthparts through which blood travels

Blood makes the abdomen look red

▲ A SATISFYING MEAL

This female mosquito has almost finished a meal of human blood. Her abdomen has swollen up like a balloon and has stretched so much that the blood inside is visible. By the time she is full, she may have five times her own weight of blood on board. People rarely feel mosquitoes biting, but they do notice the itchy feeling afterward. This happens because our bodies react to substances in mosquito saliva that make the skin around the bite become inflamed.

Sharp tip slides easily into skin

Slender legs are held out in flight

BLOODSUCKING INSECTS

HORSE FLY
The most common bloodsucking insects are two-winged flies. They include mosquitoes, black flies, and tiny midges, as well as horse flies and tsetse flies. With most of these insects, only the females suck blood, and their favorite hosts are mammals and birds. The males feed on nectar and other sugary fluids from plants.

BED BUGS
Compared to flies, only a small number of bugs feed on blood. The bed bug is one of the most notorious—thanks to the increase in human travel, it has managed to spread all around the world. Bed bugs are round and coppery colored and do not have wings. They crawl onto their hosts and always bite at night.

HUMAN HEAD LOUSE
Seen under a microscope, this human head louse shows strong claws that it uses for gripping hairs. Like all bloodsucking lice, it spends its life aboard its host, biting with sharp mouthparts on a tiny head. There are about 250 species of bloodsucking lice that live on mammals, including bats and even seals.

FLEA
With their flattened bodies and tough skins, fleas are well suited to life among feathers or fur. They do not have wings, so use their strong back legs to jump aboard their hosts. Flea larvae do not suck blood. Instead, they scavenge for food in nests and bedding, jumping onto warm-blooded animals when they become adult.

DISEASE CARRIERS

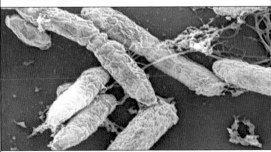

Magnified thousands of times, plague bacteria look harmless, but they can cause one of the world's deadliest diseases. The plague is spread by fleas that collect the bacteria from rats. They then bite humans, transferring the plague bacteria to them. In the past, the plague swept the world in deadly epidemics. Fortunately, antibiotics (a type of medicine) can now be used to bring it under control. Today, malaria is the most dangerous insect-borne disease. It kills millions of people every year and is spread by mosquitoes.

◄ HORSE FLY
In summer, horses are often surrounded by clouds of buzzing flies. Many of these flies are attracted by salty sweat, and they settle on horses' faces and around their eyes. These flies can be very irritating for horses, but they do not bite. Bloodsucking horse flies approach from a different angle, often landing on a horse's flanks. They cut through the skin with their bladelike jaws, and then mop up the blood that oozes out.

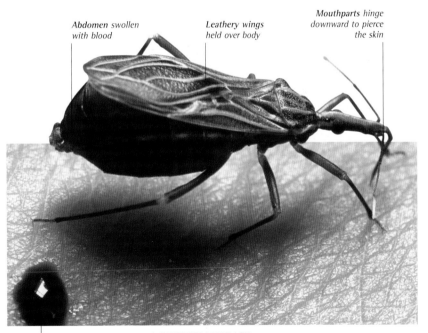

Horse fly cuts through the skin, inflicting a painful bite

Abdomen swollen with blood

Leathery wings held over body

Mouthparts hinge downward to pierce the skin

Bug excrement spreads disease if it is rubbed into the bite

▲ STEALTHY APPROACH
With its mouthparts folded downward, this assassin bug is sucking up a meal of human blood. Most assassin bugs are predators, but some types feed on blood. They often home in on a person's face and lips, which is why they are sometimes known as kissing bugs instead. Like bed bugs, they spend the day hiding away and emerge to feed at night. These bloodsuckers are unwelcome visitors because some of them spread disease.

TWO-WINGED FLIES

Many insects have the word "fly" in their name, but true flies are unique. Unlike most other flying insects, flies have two wings rather than four. This design is very efficient, and it helps to make them some of the best fliers in the insect world. Flies are extremely agile, which is why they are so difficult to swat. There are about 125,000 species of two-winged flies, and they live in every habitat on Earth. Many feed harmlessly on plants or dead remains, but this group also includes many parasites, as well as insects that suck blood and some that spread disease.

Stubby antennae pick up the scent of food

Well-developed eyes

flies

Striped thorax

TWO-WINGED FLIES ORDER

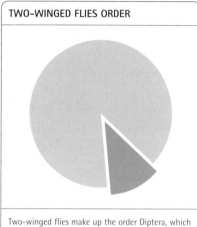

Two-winged flies make up the order Diptera, which contains about 12 percent of all known insect species. They live in many habitats, but are most common in warm and damp places. The largest are tropical mydas flies. Their wingspan—up to 10 cm (4 in)—is bigger than many butterflies.

UNWELCOME GUEST ▶
The house fly is one of the world's most widespread insects, and also a troublesome pest. Like many two-winged flies, it has a large head, short antennae, and two transparent wings. In the place of hind wings, it has two small knobs called halteres, which help to keep it balanced as it speeds through the air. House flies have good eyesight, but they track down their food mainly by its taste and smell.

Leg folds inward when fly is airborne

Hooks and suckers give fly a good grip

Transparent wings with a small number of veins

DEVELOPMENT OF A BLOW FLY

EGGS
Two-winged flies develop by complete metamorphosis – they change shape completely as they grow. The blow fly, or bluebottle, breeds on dead animals and rotting meat, finding them with its sense of smell. Female bluebottles can lay up to 500 eggs. If the weather is warm enough, the eggs hatch by the next day.

MAGGOTS
When bluebottle eggs hatch, legless larvae crawl out. These unappealing creatures— known as maggots— immediately start to feed. Maggots wriggle their way into their food, growing quickly and shedding their skin several times. After about 10 days, the maggots crawl away and turn into pupae.

PUPA
This bluebottle pupa is reddish-brown in color, with rounded ends. Inside the pupa, the maggot's body is dismantled, and an adult fly is gradually formed. This process takes about 12 days, depending on the temperature. Once the change is complete, one end of the pupa opens and a new fly crawls out.

ADULT
In as little as three weeks, the bluebottle's lifecycle is complete. Male bluebottles feed on flowers, while females lay eggs. Because bluebottles breed very quickly, they can fit many generations into a single year. In winter, the adults hibernate, but as soon as it warms up again, they reappear.

◀ WALKING UPSIDE DOWN
Many insects, such as house flies, can walk upside down. They use hooks and suckers on their feet to cling to almost any surface, including glass. Landing upside down is trickier. First, a fly catches hold with its front legs, like an acrobat grabbing a trapeze. It then swings the rest of its body underneath its legs, so that it swivels upside down. Once all six legs have made contact, it can walk around.

Lines of bristles on lower leg

◀ BRISTLY BODY
A fly's entire body, including its legs, are covered with long bristles. These bristles are very sensitive to air currents, and they warn the fly if anything is on the move nearby. Flies also have sense organs on their feet. They use these to taste things that they land on—a convenient way of finding food and good places to lay their eggs.

Reinforced veins on leading edge of wing

Wing folds back when not in use

Bristly rounded abdomen

▲ MOPPING UP
Two-winged flies all feed on liquids, but they eat in different ways. The house fly has mouthparts like a foldable sponge, and it dribbles saliva (spit) over its food. Once the food starts to dissolve, the fly sucks it up. House flies feed mainly on sugary things, although they like rotting leftovers as well. Wherever house flies land—on walls, windows, or even lightbulbs—they leave spots of sticky saliva behind.

▲ PREDATORY FLIES
Unlike house flies, robber flies catch other insects, often in midair. Once a robber fly has made its catch, it lands so that it can feed. Robber flies have sharp mouthparts and pierce their victims in a soft place, such as the neck. After sucking out the insect's juices, the robber fly discards the empty husk. Many robber flies have thick bristles on their faces to protect them against their struggling prey.

▲ BLOODSUCKING FLIES
Lots of two-winged flies live by sucking blood. They include mosquitoes, midges, horse flies, and also black flies—like the one shown here. Mosquitoes have mouthparts that work like a syringe, but horse flies and black flies bite their way through their victim's skin. Bloodsucking flies spread dangerous diseases such as malaria—not just among people, but among wild animals as well.

PARASITIC INSECTS

Instead of living on their own, parasitic insects live aboard another animal, known as their host. Fleas and lice feed on their host's blood, but other parasites have more gruesome habits—they chew or burrow into its body. They can harm their host, although the host usually survives. Parasitoids are different. They grow up inside their host, and they eat so much of it that it dies. In the insect world, parasitism is a common way of life. Some parasites can be useful, because they help to keep pests under control.

Claw hinges shut to keep a tight grip on hair

Mouthparts retract when not in use

Stubby antennae with few segments

Head lice become darker as they grow

AT HOME IN HAIR ▶
Using its hook-shaped claws, this artificially colored image of a human head louse shows it clinging to a hair. Its claws are extremely strong, which makes it very difficult to dislodge. Head lice suck blood from a person's scalp, using three slender needlelike mouthparts to pierce the skin. These tiny insects attack children more often than adults, and outbreaks are common at schools. They can be brushed or combed out, and can also be dealt with by insecticidal shampoos.

Louse climbs down hair to feed

◀ HATCHING OUT
Enlarged about 50 times, this young head louse is hatching from its egg. Female head lice lay their eggs on hairs, fastening them in place with a liquid that sets like a superhard glue. When the young louse is ready to hatch, the top of the egg falls off, and the louse squeezes its way outside. Another species, called the body louse, often lays its eggs in clothing. Unlike the head louse, it spreads a number of dangerous diseases.

◀ SEARCHING FOR A HOST
Tapping with its antennae, this ichneumon wasp tracks down its host by using smell and by sensing vibrations from larvae that feed inside plants. There are more than 60,000 species of ichneumon wasps, and almost all of them are parasitoids. Many ichneumons have a long egg-laying tube called an ovipositor that can bore through solid wood. Using this, a female ichneumon drills into tree trunks and lays her eggs inside wood-boring grubs.

◀ CATERPILLAR ATTACK
These tiny cocoons show that a caterpillar has been attacked by a parasitic wasp. The adult wasp has laid her eggs in the caterpillar and the larvae have eaten the caterpillar from inside. The larvae then crawl out of the caterpillar to pupate. A single caterpillar can provide food for more than 100 wasp larvae, which feed side by side. However, life for parasites is not completely safe, because some insects—called hyperparasites—attack parasites themselves.

◄ CUCKOO IN THE NEST ►

This beautiful African cuckoo bee does not raise its own young. Instead, it enters other bees' nests and lays its eggs inside. When its larvae hatch, they are armed with sharp jaws. They destroy all the other larvae in the nest, which leaves them with most of the food. About one-fifth of all the world's bees raise their young in this way. Adult cuckoo bees often have armored bodies, so they can survive being attacked and stung when they break into nests.

FORCED LABOR ►

Most ants are hard workers, but some species kidnap other ants and force them to work for them. This blood-red ant, shown here with its prey, is a slave-maker. It raids nearby nests and carries home the larvae of different ant species. The larvae grow up in the slave-makers' nest and behave as if they were one of them. By capturing the larvae of other workers, slave-making ants can raise more young of their own, without having to do all the work themselves.

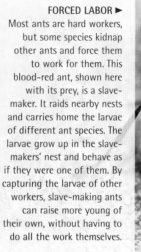

FOOD FOR A FAMILY ►

With a swift jab of its sting, this weevil-hunting wasp paralyzes its luckless prey. Instead of eating the weevil, the wasp will carry it back to its nest—a shallow burrow in the ground. Once the nest is fully stocked with weevils, the wasp will lay its eggs inside, and its larvae will use the weevils as food. Many solitary wasps collect food in this way. They carry small insects through the air, but they often drag large ones across the ground.

parasites

Strong legs grip the weevil when the wasp flies back to its nest

Good eyesight helps the wasp to locate its prey

Weevil is stung on its underside, where its exoskeleton is thinnest

STYLOPIDS

Stylopids are some of the smallest and strangest insect parasites. Males, such as this one, have bulging eyes and twisted wings. The females are wingless, legless, and blind, and live in the abdomens of bees and wasps, with just a small part of their body projecting outside. Males mate with this part, and the female produces larvae that crawl onto flowers and climb aboard new hosts, burrowing their way inside. Males eventually fly off, but females stay in their hosts.

FEEDING ON PLANTS

Every year, insects chew, nibble, and suck their way through millions of tons of plant food. No plant is safe from insect attack. Insects feast on roots, leaves, flowers, and seeds, and they also bore their way through bark and wood. With so much food available, most plant-eating insects are specialists, and their mouthparts are shaped to deal with what they eat. Many insects eat a wide range of plants, but others are extremely choosy. Some caterpillars feed on just one kind of plant.

◄ FEEDING ON SAP
After piercing a plant stem with its mouthparts, this shield bug is sucking up a meal of sap. Sap is easy to find, and it is full of sugars, which give insects the energy they need to work. However, it is low in other nutrients, particularly nitrogen, which insects need to grow. To make up for this, most sap-sucking insects spend a great deal of time feeding, particularly when they are young. Others—such as cicadas—eat less, but take much longer to grow up.

PLANT GALLS

This apple-shaped object looks like a fruit, but it is actually a growth called a gall. Galls develop when an insect lands on a plant and releases chemicals that make the plant grow. As the gall swells up, it provides the insect's young with a safe home and a source of food. Most galls are triggered by tiny wasps or midges. Each species attacks a particular plant and produces galls with a characteristic shape. This oak apple gall is soft and puffy, but some galls are woody and hard.

▲ FEEDING ON WOOD
Hidden away inside a tree trunk, these ambrosia beetle larvae are getting ready to change into adults. Ambrosia beetles bore deep into trees, leaving a network of winding tunnels behind them. Like most wood-boring beetles, they take a long time to grow up, because wood is difficult to eat, and even harder to digest. Ambrosia beetles attack a wide range of trees, including ones that are grown for their fruit.

▲ A DIET OF SEEDS
This weevil is sitting in a single grain of wheat. Its curved snout ends in a pair of small but sturdy jaws. Weevil larvae use these jaws to eat the wheat grain from the inside out. Seeds are the most nutritious parts of plants, so this single grain will keep this weevil well fed for several days. Female weevils often bore small holes in seeds and nuts with their powerful jaws, so that they can lay their eggs inside and have an immediate food source for their young. There are nearly 50,000 species of weevils, and many are pests of crops and stored food.

▲ UNDERGROUND FOOD
Mole crickets are like tunneling machines. They burrow their way through damp sand and soil, and feed by chewing through plant roots. Roots are not easy for insects to reach, but they often contain stored food. This makes them good to eat—for insects, and for humans too. Some insects, such as aphids, spend the winter sucking sap from roots, and the rest of the year above ground.

SAFETY IN NUMBERS ▶

Crowded together on a rose leaf, these buff-tip moth caterpillars are starting to feed. They will nibble their way inward from the edge of the leaf, stripping it completely before moving on to the next. During the early part of their lives, the caterpillars stick together for safety, but later on, they will go their separate ways. Moth caterpillars are some of the most voracious leaf-eaters in the insect world. Some species—like the gypsy moth—have become major pests because humans have helped them to spread.

▲ ONBOARD HELP

Plant food is easy to find, but it is not always easy to digest. Many insects get around this problem by using microorganisms. These live inside insects' intestines and release substances that break down food. These microorganisms are from the digestive system of a wood-eating termite. They swim through the termite's intestines, engulfing tiny specks of wood and turning them into food that the termite can use.

feeding on plants

Bristles and warning coloration help to deter parasites and birds

Buff-tip caterpillars eat leaves of many broad-leaved trees

▲ FUSSY EATERS

Held in place by its suckerlike prolegs, this common swallowtail caterpillar is feeding on a fennel leaf. Like many caterpillars, the common swallowtail is very particular about what it eats—fennel is its favorite food. If anything touches the caterpillar, it inflates a pair of bright red horns just behind its head. These give off a powerful smell that keeps predators at bay.

▲ FLORAL FEAST

Compared to caterpillars, earwigs are not at all particular about their food. They nibble their way through all parts of plants, including new shoots, leaves, and flowers. Unlike most plant-eating insects, they also feed on dead remains, and on any small animals that they can catch. Earwigs are not as efficient at feedling as caterpillars, but their lifestyle has one big advantage. If one kind of food runs out, they can switch to something else.

FEEDING ON FLOWERS

For many insects, flowers are perfect places for a takeout meal. The main item on the menu is nectar– a sugary liquid that is an energy-packed insect food. In return for nectar, insects carry pollen, a dust-like substance that contains a plant's male sex cells. Flowers need to exchange pollen before they can make their seeds, and the insects' delivery service gives the flowers what they need. Insects have been pollinating flowers for more than one billion years. During that time, insects and flowers have become very close partners. Some insects visit lots of different flowers and have no particular favorites, but most insects stick to ones that are the right shape for them to feed.

feeding on plants

▲ POLLEN ON THE MOVE
This photograph shows a highly magnified bee's leg. The yellow dots are grains of pollen that are trapped by microscopic hairs. The bee picks up pollen every time it visits a flower, and it delivers pollen at the same time. Bees drink lots of nectar, but they eat pollen as well. Honey bees comb it off their bodies and press it into a special basket on each hind leg so they can carry it back to their hive.

Petals attract insects toward the flower

Bee's antennae pick up the scent of a flower

Pollen carried by the bee is collected by the plant's stigmas

POLLINATION ▶
This bumble bee has just landed on a flower and is starting to feed. Many bumble bees have long tongues, and they reach deep into flowers to suck up the nectar. While the bee is feeding, the flower's anthers (male parts) dust its body with pollen. At the same time, the flower's stigmas (female parts) collect some of the pollen the bee is already carrying. Once the stigmas have collected some pollen the flower can start to make its seeds.

Bee reaches into the base of the flower to reach its nectar

Anthers dust pollen onto the bee's body

Tongue unrolls when butterfly starts to feed

Tuft of separate flowers or florets

DRINKING DEEPLY ▶
For this swallowtail butterfly, a thistle flower is a good place to feed. The flowerhead contains lots of slender flowers packed together like bristles in a brush. The butterfly unrolls its tongue and takes a drink of nectar from each. Butterflies have long tongues, but moths' can be even longer. One hawk moth from Madagascar has a 12 in (30 cm) tongue—several times longer than the rest of its body.

▲ FEEDING FLY
Using its mouthparts, this hover fly collects nectar and pollen from a flower. Unlike bees, flies do not all have long tongues, so some prefer flowers that are shallow or flat. Male hover flies often guard a patch of flowers, hovering above them in midair. The male lets females land to feed, but if a rival male appears, the first male chases him away in an aerial skirmish.

Wasp clings to flower and pushes its head inside

PERFECT FIT ▶
Instead of attracting butterflies or bees, figwort flowers are designed for wasps. This wasp has been attracted by the flower's scent and is feeding with its head inside. While it feeds, the flower dusts its chin with pollen, and the wasp carries the pollen to the next figwort flower it visits. Wasps feed their young on insects, so, unlike bees, they do not collect nectar to take back to their nests.

Holes pierced in the flower by the bee to access nectar

Meadow bumble bee clings to comfrey flower

▲ STEALING NECTAR
With its legs wrapped around a comfrey flower, this bumble bee is stealing a meal. It can smell nectar inside the flower, but its tongue is too short to reach it. Instead, the bee has cut a hole in the base of the flower so that it can reach the nectar and feed. This sneaky trick is known as nectar theft, and it is common in the insect world. Once a nectar thief has made a hole, other insects often use it too. For plants, nectar thieves are unwelcome visitors because they eat nectar without carrying pollen in return.

▲ INSECT MIMICS
Insects are not the only cheats in the pollination business. These bee orchid flowers do not produce nectar—instead, they lure male bees by smelling like females. The flowers have a furry surface, completing their disguise. When a male bee tries to pair up with its "partner," the flower clips a package of pollen onto its head. The bee flies off, and the package is collected by the next bee orchid flower it visits.

▲ SICKLY SMELLS
Most flowers attract insects with bright colors and sweet smells. This carrion flower is different because it is pollinated by flies that breed in rotting meat. It has a stomach-churning smell of decaying flesh. Female blow flies land on the flower to lay their eggs. As they walk across the petals, the flower fastens packages of pollen to their legs. When the flies visit another carrion flower, the packages are removed.

TRUE BUGS

With more than 80,000 different species, true bugs include some of the noisiest and most numerous insects in the world. Among them are ferocious predators, such as assassin bugs, and huge numbers of sap-feeders, such as tiny aphids. True bugs all have beaklike mouthparts, which they use to pierce their food, and most of them also have two pairs of wings. They live everywhere on land or in freshwater, and a few even survive on the surface of the open sea. Bugs are useful for controlling other insects, but the sap-sucking species can cause serious problems by spreading plant diseases.

true bugs

Broad head with short antennae

Hard shield at rear of head

Widely spaced eyes give cicadas a bug-eyed look

DEVELOPMENT OF AN APHID

GIVING BIRTH
Bugs develop by incomplete metamorphosis, which means that they change shape gradually as they grow. But instead of laying eggs, some kinds can give birth to live young. This female aphid has almost finished giving birth. Her baby is emerging feet-first. The baby aphid will soon be ready for its first meal.

YOUNG NYMPHS
Female aphids can produce several babies a day. Soon, each mother is surrounded by a growing family of young aphids or nymphs. Aphid nymphs look like their mothers, but they are smaller and paler. They do not have wings, but their mouthparts are fully developed, and they feed almost nonstop on plant sap.

MATURE NYMPHS
After shedding their skins several times, the nymphs look more like the adults. Each one has a small head, six spindly legs, and a large abdomen for processing sap. The nymphs can walk, but they do not wander far. As a result, space on the plant often starts to get tight, with lots of aphids feeding side by side.

WINGED ADULT
After their final molt, the aphids turn into adults. In spring and early summer, most nymphs turn into wingless females, which can breed without having to mate. Later in the year, the nymphs turn into males or females with wings. These mate, and the females fly off to lay eggs on other plants.

TROPICAL CICADA ▶
Cicadas are the largest plant-feeding bugs. Their mouthparts can fold away when not in use. They have two pairs of wings that fold back to make a shape like a sloping roof. Cicadas spend most of their lives underground, feeding on tree and shrub roots. After several years underground, they crawl up trees and turn into adults. Males attract mates by drumming plates on their abdomens—this makes a shrill call that can be heard up to a mile away.

▲ ALIEN-LOOKING BUG
Many bugs use camouflage to hide from sharp-eyed predators—particularly birds. This extraordinary treehopper, from the rain forests of South America, is adorned with two miniature antlers—one above its head, and one between its wings. The antlers help to disguise it, and make it difficult to eat. Many bugs also defend themselves by giving off an unpleasant smell if they are touched.

▲ **ASSASSIN AT WORK**
This assassin bug has caught a beetle and is finishing its meal. Like all predatory bugs, it cannot chew its food. So, it stabs its prey with its sharp beak and injects it with poisonous saliva (spit). Once its victim is dead, it feeds on the soft parts of the body, before throwing the rest away.

▲ **SAP-SUCKER**
Throughout the world, sap-sucking bugs do tremendous damage to plants. Most kinds—such as this alfafa hopper—are small, but they breed quickly when there is plenty of food. Sap-sucking bugs include aphids, mealy bugs, planthoppers, and cicadas.

▲ **UNDERWATER ATTACK**
Using its needle-sharp front legs, this giant water bug has caught a young newt. Giant water bugs lurk in muddy ponds and streams, and they can be powerful enough to stab human toes. Water boatmen and water scorpions also hunt beneath the water's surface.

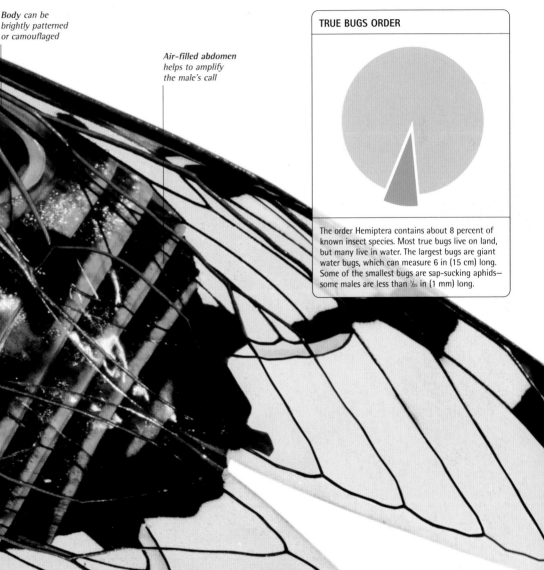

Body can be brightly patterned or camouflaged

Air-filled abdomen helps to amplify the male's call

Wings held together in an upside-down V shape when at rest

Transparent wings with strong reinforcing veins

Forewings are much longer than hind wings

TRUE BUGS ORDER

The order Hemiptera contains about 8 percent of known insect species. Most true bugs live on land, but many live in water. The largest bugs are giant water bugs, which can measure 6 in (15 cm) long. Some of the smallest bugs are sap-sucking aphids—some males are less than 1/25 in (1 mm) long.

SCAVENGERS AND RECYCLERS

Scavenging insects play an important role in the natural world. They feed on decaying organic matter, cleaning away animal droppings and removing dead bodies. They tackle leftovers and remains of every kind, breaking down their raw materials so that they can be used again and again. Most scavenging insects work after dark and find their food by smell. They live in all the world's habitats, and many of them get inside our homes. Here, the insects are less welcome, because they spoil food and some can chew their way through bedding and clothes.

Ball is patted smooth to make it roll more easily

BURIAL SQUAD ▶
This dead mouse has attracted a group of burying beetles that specialize in dealing with animal remains. Working as a team, the beetles scoop out the earth beneath the corpse, until it drops into the hole. The beetles then mate and lay their eggs there, before covering the corpse with earth. When the beetle grubs hatch, they use the mouse remains as a private larder underground.

Hind legs kick upward to roll the ball along

Beetles scoop up dung and roll it into a ball

▲ FEEDING ON DUNG
For dung beetles, this fresh pile of elephant droppings is a major find. Dung beetles feed on the droppings of plant-eating mammals, and they help to scatter dung so its nutrients are returned to the soil. They are particularly important in grasslands, because big herds of grazing mammals can produce many tons of dung each day.

ROLLING DUNG ▶
These two dung beetles have collected a pile of dung and patted it into a ball. Their next task is to roll the ball away, so that they can bury it and lay their eggs on their new food store. The beetle on the left is pushing the ball with its back legs, while its partner helps to steer. From time to time, one of the beetles climbs on top of the ball to check that it is still in shape.

OMNIVOROUS INSECTS ▶

Some insects are fussy eaters, but many cockroaches are exactly the opposite. In the wild, they feed on dead and decaying remains, but if they get indoors, they eat food and leftovers of any kind. Given the chance, they will also nibble on wallpaper paste, glue, and even soap, and they often travel inside shopping bags—an easy way of moving from place to place. Cockroaches spread diseases, contaminate food, and leave an unpleasant smell.

e ▶▶
scavengers

Oily secretions contaminate anything the cockroach walks on

Very fine hairs sense vibrations that might spell danger

Sensitive antennae pick up the scent of food

Starch-rich food attracts cockroach

Leading beetle steers the ball around obstacles

Finished ball can be as compact as a golf ball

STRANGE DIETS

CLOTHES MOTH
Clothes moth caterpillars grow up on a diet of wool. The adult moth lays her eggs on woolen clothes and blankets, and the hatched caterpillars chew small holes in them as they feed. Adult clothes moths are weak fliers, but can be transported on clothes by humans, and so are now found all around the world.

MUSEUM BEETLE
This tiny beetle can be a big problem in museums, because its grubs feed on dead insects and stuffed animals. The grubs are covered in bristles, and they chew their way through their food. In the past, these insects often ruined museum exhibits, but today deep-freezing and fumigation keep them under control.

BIRD LOUSE
Unlike bloodsucking lice, the bird louse feeds on tiny pieces of feather. It spends its entire life aboard living birds—particularly on their heads and necks, where it is safely out of reach of the birds' beaks. All wild birds are infested with these little insects, and they can be a serious pest problem on poultry farms.

INSECT DEFENSES

For insects, life is a risky business. They face attacks from other insects, and also from their archenemies—sharp-eyed birds. At the first sign of danger, most insects run or fly away to safety. Others stand their ground and rely on special defenses to survive. Camouflage makes insects difficult to see, but other defenses make them hard to get at, dangerous to touch, or extremely unpleasant to eat. If all these fail, many insects have another defensive trick—they try to bluff their way out of trouble.

protection

OFF-PUTTING EYES ▶
This male io moth defends itself by revealing a pair of large staring "eyes." The eyes are special markings on its hind wings, which the moth flashes if it is approached or touched. In the dappled light among trees, where the moth usually rests, the staring eyes look dangerous, and they can put off an attack from predators. Moths are not the only insects that have defensive eyespots—some butterflies and bugs have them too.

Each eyespot has a black pupil— just like a real eye

Wings open fully to reveal eyespots

Hairs break away easily if they are touched

Dense tuft of brown hairs at end of abdomen

Long sharp-tipped hairs grow in all directions

Four dense tufts of pale hairs along back

Double row of short barbed hairs on either side of back

BRISTLY MEAL ▶
With its extraordinary bristles and tufts of hair, the vaporer moth caterpillar looks more like a set of brushes than a living insect. This particular caterpillar is facing forward—its head is hidden, but a long tuft of grey bristles sticks out on each side. Vaporer moth caterpillars feed out in the open, and they use their bristles to keep birds at bay. Like many bristly caterpillars, they can trigger skin rashes in humans if they are touched.

SITTING TARGET ▶
Removed from its protective froth, this young spittlebug nymph is easy prey for other insects and for birds. Its body is pale and soft, its legs are too weak for it to run away. Instead, it relies on its froth for protection. When it becomes an adult, it develops a much tougher body and stronger legs. It leaves its froth, and escapes from danger by jumping from plant to plant.

Spittlebug nymph walking back into its froth

▲ HIDE AND SEEK
Young spittlebugs feed by sucking sap, and they live in the open on plants. To protect themselves from attack, they hide in a jacket of froth, which forms like bubbles in a foamy bath. Here, a green spittlebug nymph is making its way back into its protective froth. Spittlebug nymphs make their froth from sap that they have swallowed and digested. As the froth dries out, a spittlebug makes more, so its defensive hideaway always stays filled up.

Bold warning colors instead of camouflage keep away prey

Bubbles give off a powerful smell when they burst

Weak wings mean that the grasshopper is a poor flier

Froth contains mucus mixed with water from digested sap

Joint between thorax and abdomen can move with a sudden snap

LAST RESORT ▶
In an emergency, some insects use tricks that can save their lives. Many shed some of their legs, but some go even further, by pretending to be dead. With luck, the predator loses interest. Once it has gone, the insect quickly comes back to life. Click beetles add their own special twist to this common defense technique. After playing dead for several seconds, they snap a special joint between their thorax and abdomen. The force is so strong that it hurls the beetle into the air.

Legs fold away into recesses on the beetle's underside

Long bullet-shaped body

UNPALATABLE PROSPECT ▲
If it is threatened, this African grasshopper does not try to hop or fly away. Instead, it produces a mass of evil-smelling froth from holes in the thorax. The smell alone is enough to keep most predators away, but if anything does try to eat the grasshopper, the taste is even worse. Grasshoppers—and many other insects—get their defensive chemicals from the plants that they eat. These insects often have bright colors as an extra defense—to warn away other animals.

CLICK BEETLE ESCAPE BEHAVIOR

PLAYING DEAD
If a click beetle is threatened, it lies on its back with its legs pulled in and pretends to be dead. Most predators hunt by looking for movement, so after a few seconds, the beetle's enemy often goes away.

LIFTOFF
If the beetle is still in danger, it tenses its muscles, and the joint between its thorax and abdomen clicks, making its thorax smash against the ground. This movement throws the beetle skyward.

LANDING
With its legs still tucked in, the beetle travels up to 12 in (30 cm) through the air. Seconds later, it crash-lands. As soon as it hits the ground, it turns the right way up, extends its legs, and runs away.

CAMOUFLAGE AND MIMICRY

Insects are experts in the art of disguise. For millions of years, they have used camouflage and mimicry to help them survive. Camouflage makes insects blend in with their background—whether it is bark or featureless desert sand. Mimicry works in a different way, because the insect does not try to hide. Instead, it copies something inedible, or something that predators would avoid. Insects mimic all kinds of objects, such as twigs, and harmless species mimic those that have poisonous bodies or stings. The result is a confusing world, where nothing is quite what it seems.

camouflage

SNAKE MIMIC ▶
From a distance, this hawk moth caterpillar looks amazingly like a snake. With its head tucked away and the front of its body hunched up, its shows off its glaring "eyes." To make the performance even more realistic, the caterpillar waves from side to side. A closer look reveals that this is not a snake because it has several pairs of legs. But for most predators, just one glance is enough. The threat of being bitten makes them stay away.

False midrib runs across forewings and hind wings

Eyespots face toward the front

◀ LIFE IN DEAD LEAVES
Crouched on the end of a twig, this Indian leaf butterfly mimics a dead leaf. Here, the butterfly is facing toward the right, with its wings folded together behind its body. Its wings have a dark band that looks like a leaf's midrib, and they are exactly the right color to blend in with the dead leaves around them. In flight, the butterfly looks very different, because the upper surfaces of its wings are colored orange and blue.

◀ LEAVES THAT WALK
Unlike the Indian leaf butterfly, this insect mimics living leaves. It is a leaf insect—one of about 30 species that live in Southeast Asia and Australia. Leaf insects are green or brown, and they have a flat abdomen that looks uncannily like a real leaf. To complete the disguise, this leaf insect has flaps on its legs, and it moves slowly, swaying gently with the breeze. Like other leaf insects, it feeds at night, when fewer predators are on the move.

Real head is tucked away in the shadows

Front body segments contract to produce a shape like a snake's head

THE PERFECT DISGUISE ▶
Some of the best insect mimics are those that copy bees and wasps. This harmless clearwing moth mimics a hornet—an extra-large wasp armed with a powerful sting. The moth's mimicry is astoundingly good. Just like a real hornet, it has yellow and brown markings, a narrow waist, and transparent wings. It feeds by day, making a loud buzzing sound as it flies. With its menacing looks, the moth fools most people, and most birds as well.

Scales fall off wings during the moth's first flight, leaving them clear

CLEARWING MOTH

HORNET

Body has warning colors

POISONOUS LOOK ▶
In North America, the viceroy butterfly protects itself by copying another species— the black and orange monarch. Unlike the viceroy, the monarch is packed with poisons that it collects from its milkweed foodplant. Any bird that tries to eat a monarch is very quickly sick. Birds soon learn this, and they leave monarchs alone. The viceroy is harmless, but because it resembles the monarch, birds avoid it as well. This kind of mimicry is common among butterflies— some poisonous species are copied by dozens of harmless species.

Wing shape and color resemble a monarch's

MONARCH BUTTERFLY

VICEROY BUTTERFLY

LIVING THORNS ▶
Thorn bugs have long spines that stick up above their backs. The spine protects them in two different ways—it makes them look like part of a plant, but also, if a predator does spot them, it makes them harder to eat. Thorn bugs feed on plant sap, and they often live in groups. They spread out along a stem, all facing the same way, which makes them look even more like genuine plant thorns.

DEADLY TWIGS ▶
Anchored by its prolegs, this geometrid moth caterpillar looks like a twig. Its skin is the color of bark, and it points in the right direction, slanting away from a branch. Most geometrid caterpillars use this camouflage to hide from birds, but some use it for more sinister reasons. If another insect comes within range, they catch it and eat it— a rare example of caterpillars feeding on animal prey.

BIRD DROPPINGS ▶
Few animals eat bird droppings, so looking like one is a good way of surviving. This caterpillar uses this grotesque disguise. Its body is gray with splashes of white— just like a real dropping that has landed on a leaf. Caterpillars often mimic bird droppings when they are young. As they get bigger, they often change color, so that they blend in with the leaves around them instead.

HIDING ON BARK ▶
The peppered moth blends with its background when it rests on bark. This moth is a famous example of evolution in action. In Great Britain, dark-winged forms became common during the 1800s, when coal fires blackened trees with soot. The dark-winged moths were harder for birds to spot than ones with lighter wings. As a result, they had a better chance of surviving and reproducing.

CRICKETS AND GRASSHOPPERS

Compared to some insects, crickets and grasshoppers are easy to recognize. They have sturdy bodies and two pairs of wings, and extra-large back legs. If danger threatens, they give a powerful kick, throwing themselves several yards through the air. The males are also tireless singers. Male grasshoppers sing by rubbing their hind legs against their bodies, but male crickets rub their front wings together instead. Most crickets and grasshoppers feed on plants. On their own, they do little damage, but swarming species—called locusts—can devastate crops.

Long antennae are a feature of crickets

Antennae are very fine with many segments

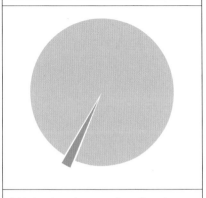

CRICKETS AND GRASSHOPPERS ORDER

Crickets and grasshoppers make up the order Orthoptera, which contains about 2 percent of all known insect species. This order includes some of the world's largest and heaviest insects. One species—the flightless wetapunga from New Zealand—weighs up to 3 oz (70 g).

▼ GREEN FOR SAFETY

Crickets and grasshoppers often use camouflage to avoid being seen. This female great green bushcricket from Europe blends in perfectly against bright green leaves. Her bladelike egg-laying tube, called an ovipositor, makes her look dangerous, but although she can bite, she cannot sting. Like most crickets, she has long thin antennae and fingerlike mouthparts (palps) that feel her food. Her wings are well developed, but many crickets have much smaller wings, or even no wings at all. Katydids are also known as bushcrickets.

Transparent wings with green veins

Two pairs of well-developed wings

Large eyes

CRICKET CANNIBALS

Unlike grasshoppers, many crickets have a taste for animals. They catch prey with their front legs and then crunch it up with their powerful jaws. This cricket has caught another one that came too close. It will eat most of its body, letting the legs and wings drop to the ground. Many crickets have a cannibal streak. Young crickets have to take care if larger ones are nearby.

Palps

Ear on front leg

Spiracle on thorax

Tibia (lower leg) has rows of spikes

Large muscle-packed femur of hind leg

Abdomen expands and contracts to help cricket breathe

Strong claws

crickets

Knee straightens suddenly when cricket jumps

LOCUST DEVELOPMENT

EGGS
Crickets and grasshoppers develop by incomplete metamorphosis (they change shape gradually as they grow up). They start life as eggs. These eggs have been laid by a locust. Using her abdomen like a digger, the mother has buried her eggs an inch or so deep in moist sand.

YOUNG NYMPH
When locust eggs hatch, the young look like small stubby worms. They wriggle their way to the surface and immediately shed their skins. After this first molt, they are young nymphs or hoppers, with well-developed legs. Hoppers cannot fly, but armies of them can hop a long way in search of a meal.

FINAL MOLT
As a locust hopper grows up, it sheds its skin six times. Each time it does this, it clings firmly to a twig, and its old skin splits down the back. The hopper then pulls itself free, leaving the empty skin behind. Before locusts start to swarm, the ground is covered with millions of hoppers, molting and searching for food.

ADULT
After the final molt, an adult emerges. Unlike a hopper, it has fully working wings and is ready to breed. Locusts fly well. When their food starts to run out, the adults take to the air in a swarm. A single swarm can contain over a billion locusts—they look like dark snowflakes fluttering through the sky.

◄ FEEDING ON FLOWERS
Grasshoppers are vegetarians, but grass makes up only a small part of their food. Many prefer other kinds of low-growing plants, and some specialize in feeding on certain shrubs. Grasshoppers also like to eat flowers. This grasshopper has climbed onto a flower and is starting to feed. It grips its food tightly with its front legs and then lowers its jaws to munch through the petals.

Leaves and petals make a good meal for grasshoppers

Hind wing opens out like a fan during flight

SCAVENGING AFTER DARK ▲
When night falls, scavenging crickets come out to feed. This Jerusalem cricket eats other insects, as well as plant roots, and dead plant and animal remains. Unlike katydids, scavenging crickets spend most of their time on the ground. Many dig burrows in loose earth, where they hide away during the day. Cave crickets are also scavengers, but they live underground full-time.

Long ovipositor for laying eggs

INSECT REPRODUCTION

Insects are incredibly good at breeding, which is one of the reasons why they are such successful animals. If conditions are good, they can build up huge numbers in a short space of time. Fortunately, these population booms rarely last for long, but it only takes a handful of parents to make them start. For most insects, breeding begins with courtship, and it really gets under way when the parents mate. After that, the young start out on life, growing fast and changing shape as they head toward adulthood themselves.

SEASONAL REPRODUCTION

Shrouded in a net, this visitor to the Arctic tundra has attracted a cloud of hungry mosquitoes, eager for a meal of blood. In the Arctic, insects have only a few weeks in which to breed. From late spring onward, billions of mosquitoes take to the air, making life uncomfortable for people and wild animals. The mosquitoes mate and lay their eggs, and by late summer, when the temperature starts to drop dramatically, most of them are dead.

Young grasshoppers often crowd together for safety

◀ YOUNG GRASSHOPPERS

A few days after hatching, these young lubber grasshoppers are chewing their way through a lantana plant. Grasshoppers lay lots of eggs, so their numbers can soar if their young have enough food. However, each of these hoppers has only a small chance of becoming a parent itself. Some will die from hunger, or from disease. A few will die through accidents, while eating or on the move. Many will be caught and eaten by predators—including other insects.

Hopper holds a leaf by both sides to feed

Hopper finds food by walking

▼ POPULATION EXPLOSION

With the help of a calculator, it is easy to see why insects can outbreed many other animals. Here, two parent weevils produce 80 young. If all the young survive to lay eggs, they will have 3,200 offspring of their own. By the third generation, there will be 128,000 weevils, if they still have enough to eat. By the 18th generation, if conditions were favorable, there would be so many weevils that they would fill the entire volume of the Earth.

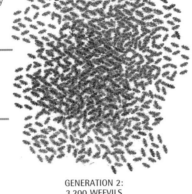

PARENT WEEVILS

GENERATION 1:
80 WEEVILS

GENERATION 2:
3,200 WEEVILS

GENERATION 3:
128,000 WEEVILS

MALES AND FEMALES

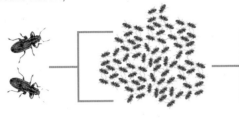

reproduction

MALE BANDED DEMOISELLE
Male and female insects often look identical and it takes an expert eye to tell them apart. In some species—such as damselflies—the difference is easy to see. This banded demoiselle has an electric blue body and a smoky patch on its wings. Only the males have these colors and markings.

FEMALE BANDED DEMOISELLE
Compared to the male, the female looks as if she belongs to a different species. Her wings are clear and her body is green. These color differences are also shown by some dragonflies and butterflies. Normally, the male has the brightest colors—he uses them during courtship to attract a mate.

Sharp mouthparts of female tsetse fly

Larva emerging from female's abdomen

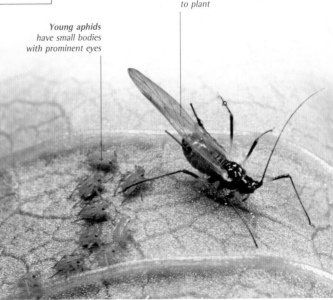

Young aphids have small bodies with prominent eyes

Winged adult aphids spread from plant to plant

▲ LAYING A LARVA

Most insects breed by laying eggs, but bloodsucking tsetse flies produce living larvae instead. This female has nearly finished giving birth to a larva that is almost half her size. Unusually for an insect, the mother nourishes the larva while it is in her body, and the larva turns into a pupa soon after it is laid. The adult will produce about a dozen offspring in her six month lifespan. Tsetse flies live in Africa and spread disease to cattle and humans when they feed.

▲ GIVING BIRTH

In spring and summer, aphids give birth to live young. Here a cluster of recently born aphids are dwarfed by a winged adult, on the right. Female aphids can give birth to several young a day. They do not have to mate in order to breed, because their eggs develop without having to be fertilized by the males. Giving birth to live young allows the females to raise families quickly, without having to move away from their food. Aphids feed on plant sap.

COURTSHIP AND MATING

Insects often spend a long time growing up, but much less time as adults. Once they have grown up, most species set about finding a partner as quickly as they can. Insects do this by using special courtship behavior that brings the males and females together. Some insects perform courtship dances, while others produce flashes of light or bursts of sound. Many females give off a scent—males can sometimes smell this nearly a mile away. Once the two partners meet, they pair up and mate. For the female, the next task is laying eggs.

Legs are blurred as they rub up and down

◄ SIGNALING WITH LIGHT

When night falls, fireflies switch on organs that give off an eerie greenish light. The males weave their way through the air, signaling to females hiding in bushes, or in the grass below. When a female flashes back, the male drops down to mate. Each species of firefly uses its own call sign. However, some fireflies cheat—the females copy the flashes of other fireflies, and eat the males when they come in to land.

▲ SCRAPING A SONG

This grasshopper is calling to females by rubbing his hind legs against his wings. The inside of his legs have tiny pegs that scrape on the wings' veins. The result is a loud buzz—a characteristic sound in grassy places on a summer's day. This way of producing sound is called stridulation. Crickets also stridulate, but instead of using their legs, they sing by scraping their wings together. Many crickets sing late into the night.

Female fireflies are hidden in long grass

Males signal to females on the ground

Male injects sperm into the female's reproductive system

Female and male are locked together when they mate

▲ HOW INSECTS MATE

In insects, mating can be a drawn-out business. These two shield bugs are mating, and will stay joined for several hours. Once they have finished, the male's sperm will fertilize the female's eggs, so that they are ready to be laid. Insects mate in many different ways. Bugs usually pair up back-to-back, but many other insects face forward. Dragonflies pair up by arching their bodies around each other to make a shape like a heart.

BUTTERFLY COURTSHIP

SCENT SIGNALS

At short range, butterflies make contact by sight, but at long range they use scent. This female Indonesian handkerchief butterfly is giving out scent as she flies. As the scent disperses, it is picked up by male butterflies, who head upwind to find her. Male butterflies sense the female's scent with their antennae.

FLYPAST

A male has found the female by picking up her scent, and starts his courtship dance around her. He swoops under and past the female, showering her with his own scent, which is produced by special scales on his wings. The female flies on, but she watches his dance closely, and she picks up his scent.

PAIRING UP

As the dance continues, the male circles around the female. His scent and his movements show the female that he belongs to the right species, and that he would make a suitable partner. After watching his dance for a short while, she settles on a leaf. The male lands beside her and they mate.

FATAL MATING ►

Predatory insects have to take extra care when they mate—particularly if they are male. This female praying mantis has captured her smaller male partner and is eating his thorax and head. The male has already mated with her, and his body will serve as a nutritious food for her to form her eggs. However, male mantises do not always meet this fate. Sometimes the female has recently fed, so the male can mate and then quickly make his getaway.

mating

▼ FENDING OFF RIVALS

Using his massive jaws, one of these stag beetles has lifted the other into the air. Both are males fighting for a chance to mate. In the insect world, fights between males are common, particularly when males defend a private courtship territory. These fights look dangerous, but the losers usually survive. However, in stag beeetles, the defeated male's cuticle (body case) is often damaged, and so he will not be able to reproduce.

"Antlers" are modified jaws, found only in males

Thorax hinges upward to lift the opponent in the air

Hind legs brace the beetle's body

EGGS AND YOUNG

Insect eggs are tiny, but they are some of the most intricate objects in the animal world. They come in many different shapes, and their shells are often sculptured with ribs and spikes. Insect eggs are extremely tough, but they are also living things, which means that they have to breathe. Their shells let air flow in and out, but they keep water inside, so that the egg does not dry out. Some eggs hatch within days, while others wait for months until outside conditions are just right. After breaking the shell or biting through it, a young insect crawls out.

PERFECTLY PLACED ▶
Magnified over a hundred times, the eggs of the cabbage white butterfly look like neatly stacked corn cobs. The female lays her eggs on the underside of cabbage leaves, in batches of several dozen. Each female takes great care about where she lay her eggs because her caterpillars are fussy eaters. Before she lays, she tastes the leaves with her feet, searching for the chemicals that give cabbage its bitter flavor.

Transparent shell left behind after caterpillar has hatched

Unhatched egg containing developing caterpillar

◀ SAFETY IN STRINGS
The map butterfly lays its eggs in strings, fastened to the underside of nettle leaves. Each string contains up to a dozen eggs—here, some of them have hatched, and the caterpillars are setting off to feed. Laying eggs in strings helps to disguise them from predatory birds. Map butterflies produce two generations a year. Adults in the first generation look different from the ones in the second.

Fleshy horns at the tip of each egg

◀ EGG CLUTCHES
Most insects lay eggs in groups called clutches. This clutch was laid by a female leaf beetle. When eggs are laid in clutches, instead of separately, the young insects start life together. Sometimes they stay together until they are adult. More often, they split up when their food starts to run low in order to find food elsewhere. Not all the young will survive to adulthood.

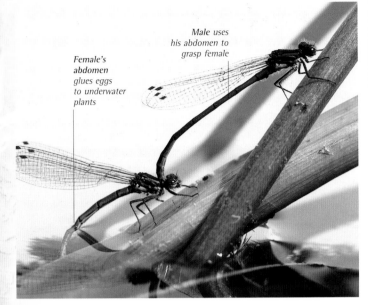

Female's abdomen *glues eggs to underwater plants*

Male uses *his abdomen to grasp female*

eggs

▲ LAYING EGGS

With her neck clasped by her partner, this female damselfly is laying her eggs in a pond. In most insects—apart from damselflies—the female lays on her own. Butterflies glue their eggs to plants, but many stick insects drop them on the ground. Grasshoppers bury them underground, while praying mantises lay them in a foam package, which hardens to form a case.

▲ IDEAL HOME

Gripping a leaf with its legs, this Costa Rican butterfly is laying a batch of eggs. Before she lays, she checks the leaf closely to make sure that it has not been used before. If she spots another female's eggs—or if she senses their smell—she will fly away and lay her own eggs on another plant. This behaviour helps her caterpillars, because it means they have a food supply all to themselves.

PARENTAL CARE

Small hole *shows that the egg is beginning to hatch*

Caterpillar *emerging from egg*

GIANT WATER BUG
Most insects abandon their eggs once they have been laid and leave them to develop on their own. Bugs are different, because they often protect their young. This giant water bug is a male. After mating, the female has glued her eggs onto his back. The male carries the eggs and guards them until they hatch.

SHIELD BUG
This shield bug's eggs have hatched, and the mother is guarding her young. If danger threatens, the young cluster beneath her, like chicks under a hen. The mother does not feed them, but she continues to stand guard until her young can look after themselves. This usually takes about two to three days.

◀ HATCHING

Clustered together on a heather stem, these emperor moth caterpillars have just hatched from their eggs. To hatch, each caterpillar chews a hole in the top of the egg, and then gradually wriggles out. Many newly hatched insects start life by eating their egg's shell. Insect egg shells are rich in protein, so they make a nutritious first meal.

GROWING UP

Once an insect has hatched, it starts feeding and begins to grow. As its size increases, it periodically molts (sheds) its exoskeleton. Each time this happens, its body changes shape. In some insects, such as dragonflies and bugs, the changes are gradual and minimal. This is known as incomplete metamorphosis. The young—called nymphs— look very much like their parents, although they do not have wings. In other insects, such as butterflies and beetles, the changes are far more drastic, and they happen in a special resting stage called a pupa. This is called complete metamorphosis, and the insects change shape completely.

e▶▶
changing shape

▲ BECOMING AN ADULT
This cicada is shedding its skin for the final time and turning into an adult. The old skin splits open along its back, and the adult cicada climbs out. At first its body is pale and soft, and its wings are crumpled. After a few hours, its body hardens, and its wings spread out. Most insects—aside from silverfish and mayflies—stop molting once they are adult. After their final molt, their shape does not change any more.

▼ INCOMPLETE METAMORPHOSIS
Dragonfly nymphs live in ponds and lakes, and they stay underwater for up to three years. Eventually, during a warm day in spring or early summer, each nymph crawls out of the water to start its adult life. Here, a nymph has climbed to the top of a plant stem. Gripping the stem firmly with its legs, it begins its amazing transformation from a sluggish freshwater insect into a fast-flying adult dragonfly.

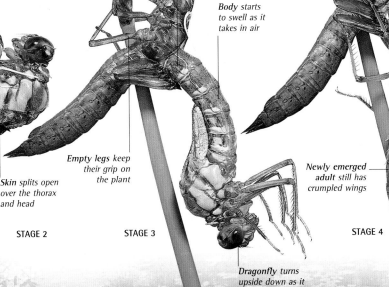

Legs lock around plant stem

Skin splits open over the thorax and head

Empty legs keep their grip on the plant

Abdomen slides out of skin

Body starts to swell as it takes in air

Dragonfly turns upside down as it emerges

Newly emerged adult still has crumpled wings

STAGE 1 STAGE 2 STAGE 3 STAGE 4

◄ ADULT DRAGONFLY

Two hours after it emerged from the water, the dragonfly is now an adult and ready to take to the air. Its body has expanded and is now twice as long as the empty skin, which is still firmly attached to the plant. Its wing veins have filled with blood, making the wings spread out, and its head has also changed shape. The nymph's eyes have been transformed into ones that work in air instead of water, and its mouthparts have changed into biting jaws. The nymph was camouflaged, but the adult has iridescent colors that glint in the sunlight.

Powerful bristly legs

Wing veins support the wings as they beat up and down

Wings harden after they have expanded

STAGE 5

Colors gradually change as the adult matures

Long abdomen balances the dragonfly as it flies

INCOMPLETE METAMORPHOSIS IN OTHER INSECTS

MAYFLY NYMPH

ADULT MAYFLY

MAYFLIES
Like dragonflies, mayflies grow up underwater, but their adult life often lasts less than one day. Mayflies are unique in another way, because they molt for a second time after they have developed wings. The adults emerge in large swarms that fly over water, scattering their eggs before they die.

GRASSHOPPER NYMPH

ADULT GRASSHOPPER

GRASSHOPPERS
Young grasshoppers look very much like their parents, although their bodies are shorter and stubbier, and they do not have working wings. Each time they molt, their wing buds grow bigger, until they reach adult size. In total, grasshoppers usually molt between four and six times.

COCKROACH NYMPH

ADULT COCKROACH

COCKROACHES
Young cockroaches are wingless, and in some species, the adults are as well. When the nymphs hatch, they have wormlike bodies, but from their first molt onward, they look much more like adults. Altogether, cockroaches molt up to 12 times, over a period of several months.

MANTIS NYMPH

ADULT MANTIS

PRAYING MANTISES
Like cockroaches, newly hatched praying mantises have a wormlike shape, although this does not last for long. Within days and after several molts, they become much more like the adults, with a lean body and grasping front legs. Most species molt between eight and 12 times before they become adults.

TERMITE NYMPH

ADULT REPRODUCTIVE

TERMITES
These insects take up to a year to become adult. They molt up to 10 times, but when they become adult, only potential kings and queens have wings. Known as reproductives, they use them to fly away and start new nests. Adult worker and soldier termites are wingless.

CHANGING SHAPE

There is no such thing as a baby butterfly, a baby beetle, or a baby fly. Instead, these insects lead two quite separate lives. An insect spends the first part as a larva, which is little more than an eating machine. Once it has eaten its fill, the larva enters a special resting stage called a pupa. During the following days or weeks, the larva's body is broken down, and an adult body with an entirely different shape is assembled in its place. This incredible transformation is called complete metamorphosis.

e▸▸
changing
shape

SETTLING DOWN

Silk pad glued to twig anchors the caterpillar

CHRYSALIS

Caterpillar skin splits and peels away to reveal chrysalis

▲ **COMPLETE METAMORPHOSIS**
This caterpillar is the larva of a monarch butterfly. After feeding and growing for several weeks, it stops eating and hangs upside down from a silk pad. It then turns into a pupa, which is covered by a case called a chrysalis. Once the chrysalis is complete, metamorphosis begins. After about 10 days, the chrysalis splits open, and the adult butterfly crawls out.

Soft chrysalis begins to harden in the air

◄ **MIMICKING A DEAD LEAF**
During their transformation, most pupae cannot move. To escape predators, some butterflies and moths pupate underground, but others rely on camouflage. The cruiser butterfly from Asia has a chrysalis that looks like a dead leaf. Blotches and wispy edges help the pupa to blend into the background. Other butterfly species mimic twigs, leaves, or bird droppings.

Irregular shape imitates a decayed leaf skeleton

◄ **POISONOUS CHRYSALIS**
The queen butterfly of North and Central America has a chrysalis that is clearly marked with a bright yellow stripe. As a caterpillar, the queen feeds on milkweeds and milkweed vines, plants with poisons in their sap. The queen stores these poisons, called glycosides, in its body. Predators that try to eat the caterpillar, the chrysalis, or the adult are immediately sick. The bright color reminds a predator to avoid eating a queen next time it finds one.

Vivid color is a warning to predators

COMPLETE METAMORPHOSIS IN OTHER INSECTS

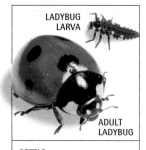

LADYBUG LARVA

ADULT LADYBUG

BEETLE
Some beetle larvae have tiny legs, or even no legs at all. Ladybug larvae do have them, and they crawl over plants to find their food. During their metamorphosis, they change shape completely, developing brightly colored forewings that arch over their backs.

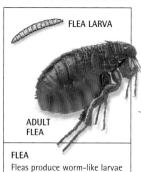

FLEA LARVA

ADULT FLEA

FLEA
Fleas produce worm-like larvae that live in nests or bedding material. The adult flea develops inside a pupa, but does not hatch straight away. It waits until it senses the movement of a host animal, then breaks open the pupal case, and jumps aboard.

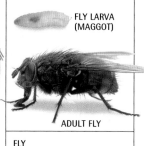

FLY LARVA (MAGGOT)

ADULT FLY

FLY
Fly larvae are legless, and they often burrow through their food. Some feed on fungi or rotting plants, but bluebottle larvae grow up on meat. When they are mature, they wriggle away from the corpse and find somewhere cool and dry to pupate.

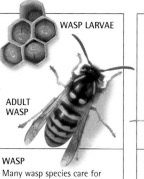

WASP LARVAE

ADULT WASP

WASP
Many wasp species care for their larvae in specially built paper cells. Eggs are placed at the bottom of the cell. Adults bring meat to each larva, which gradually grows until it fills its cell. When the larva is ready, it seals itself inside the cell and pupates.

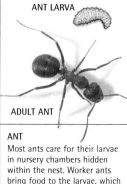

ANT LARVA

ADULT ANT

ANT
Most ants care for their larvae in nursery chambers hidden within the nest. Worker ants bring food to the larvae, which wave their heads from side to side to beg for food. Ant larvae pupate inside a cocoon of silk. The pupae are often mistaken for ant eggs.

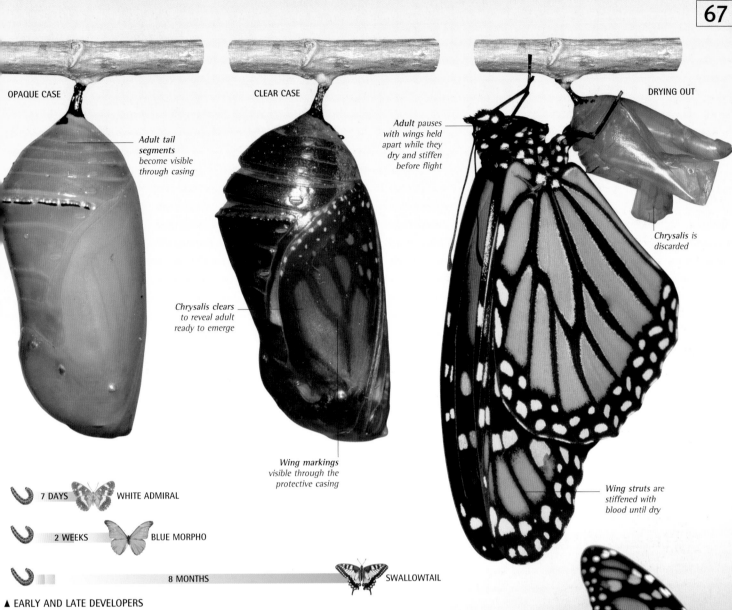

OPAQUE CASE

Adult tail segments become visible through casing

CLEAR CASE

Chrysalis clears to reveal adult ready to emerge

Wing markings visible through the protective casing

Adult pauses with wings held apart while they dry and stiffen before flight

DRYING OUT

Chrysalis is discarded

Wing struts are stiffened with blood until dry

7 DAYS — WHITE ADMIRAL

2 WEEKS — BLUE MORPHO

8 MONTHS — SWALLOWTAIL

▲ EARLY AND LATE DEVELOPERS

Most butterflies take a few weeks to turn into adults. Sometimes, three or four generations can follow each other in one year. But not all butterflies breed this quickly. Some overwinter—hibernating in a sheltered place until they can lay eggs the following spring. Others use the pupa as their dormant stage. In some swallowtails, the pupa can last for many months.

LIQUID FOOD ►

A caterpillar's mouth has cutting and chewing parts designed for eating plant leaves, but the adult mouthparts, which develop inside the pupa, make a proboscis (tube-shaped tongue). The adult butterfly uses this to suck up sugary nectar from flowers. Nectar is a very efficient fuel for flying, but it does not contain any proteins, so adult butterflies cannot grow or repair themselves if their bodies get damaged.

UNDERGROUND MOTH PUPA

Many moths pupate underground or buried in leaf litter. The caterpillar creates a hollow in the soil. A few moth species coat the walls of the chamber with silk, to keep out the damp and the cold. Silk also clogs the mouthparts of some small predators, making moth pupae less desirable as food. Most moth pupae simply form a tough chrysalis. As the pupa matures, features such as the eyes, antennae, and tail become visible inside the chrysalis.

BUTTERFLIES AND MOTHS

With their beautiful colors and broad wings, butterflies are eye-catching insects. Like moths, they feed on sugary fluids, sipping them up with tube-shaped tongues. Their larvae (called caterpillars) are very different. They have tough jaws, and usually feed on plants. Adult butterflies and moths are covered with tiny scales. Moth scales are usually dull and drab, but butterfly scales can be as vivid as specks of paint. Butterflies fly and feed during the day, while most moths fly by night.

e►►
butterflies

Slender threadlike antennae with club-shaped tips

Wings are spread to soak up the sun's warmth

Silky hairs help to insulate the butterfly's body

BUTTERFLIES AND MOTHS ORDER

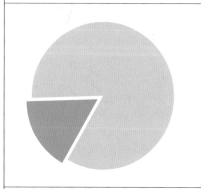

There are more than 160,000 species of butterfly and moth. They make up the order Lepidoptera, which contains 16.5 percent of the world's known insects. Some species are large and very colorful, but the order also contains thousands of micromoths—tiny insects that often go unnoticed.

▲ REFUELING STOP
This European swallowtail butterfly has landed on a flower to feed. Like all butterflies, it has two pairs of wings that are covered with overlapping scales. Scales also cover the rest of its body—on its abdomen they are long and silky like fur. Butterflies have well-developed eyes, and slender antennae with club-shaped tips. Many butterflies are strong fliers, and some moths are as well. Every year, some species migrate thousands of miles to reach suitable places to breed.

Eyespot diverts attacking birds away from the butterfly's head

Tailed hind wings are a characteristic feature of swallowtail butterflies

Thickened veins strengthen the leading edge of the wings

Forewings are larger than the hind wings

Case protects the caterpillar as it feeds

Scales contain chemical pigments that give them vivid colors

MOTH OR BUTTERFLY?

MOTH
Moths usually have dull colors to camouflage them during the day. Most rest with their wings spread flat or—like this oak eggar moth—sloping over their bodies like a roof. Typically, antennae are thick, without a swelling at the tip. Some moths are active during the day.

BUTTERFLY
In typical butterfly fashion, this monarch holds its wings upright, except when it is basking in the sun. In general, butterflies are brightly colored and much easier to spot than moths. However, some have camouflaged underwings, which they use to hide beneath when they rest.

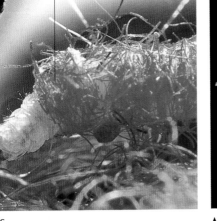

▲ UNUSUAL DIETS
This clothes moth caterpillar is chewing its way through a woolen blanket. It lives inside a portable case, made of strands of wool held together by silk. Most butterfly caterpillars feed on leaves, but moth caterpillars have more varied diets—as well as wool, some chew their way through nuts and seeds, and a few even catch other insects.

▲ ROLL-OUT TONGUES
Hovering in front of an orchid at night, this hawk moth is using its enormous tongue to reach the nectar inside the flower. Its tongue is far longer than its body, and it works like an extra-fine drinking straw. When the moth finishes feeding it rolls up its tongue like a tightly coiled spring and flies away. Keeping its tongue out when flying would use up too much energy.

DEVELOPMENT OF A RED ADMIRAL BUTTERFLY

EGG
Like all butterflies, red admirals start life as eggs. The eggs are green, with white vertical ribs, and the females lay them singly on the leaves of stinging nettle plants. Red admiral butterfly eggs hatch after about a week. The caterpillar emerges and makes itself a shelter like a tent by folding over the leaf with silk.

CATERPILLAR
Red admiral caterpillars are either black or yellowish-brown, with two rows of bristly spikes running along their backs. As they grow, they make a series of leaf-tents to hide from birds and other predators. From time to time the caterpillar emerges from its tent to make a new home or to feed.

PUPA
Once it has finished growing, the caterpillar turns into a pupa that hangs from a nettle stem. The pupa or chrysalis (case) is shiny and hardens soon after it forms. The pupa takes about 10 days to turn into an adult butterfly. The bright colors inside this chrysalis show that the change is almost complete.

ADULT
Eventually, the chrysalis splits open and the adult butterfly crawls out. Adult red admirals feed and mate from late spring to early fall, or even later if the weather is warm. When it turns cold, they hibernate. The survivors emerge in spring and start laying eggs, and so the cycle begins again.

INSECT LIFESPANS

Compared to mammals or birds, insects have varied lifespans. The shortest-lived insects are tiny wasps and flies. In favorable conditions, some of these hatch, grow, breed, and die within two weeks. Many of these fast breeders are parasites, while others live on food that disappears quickly, such as rotting fruit. However, wood-boring beetles can live for over a decade, while queen termites can live for 50 years. During her long life, a queen termite enjoys one brief flight. After that, she spends the rest of her time deep in a nest, locked inside a royal cell.

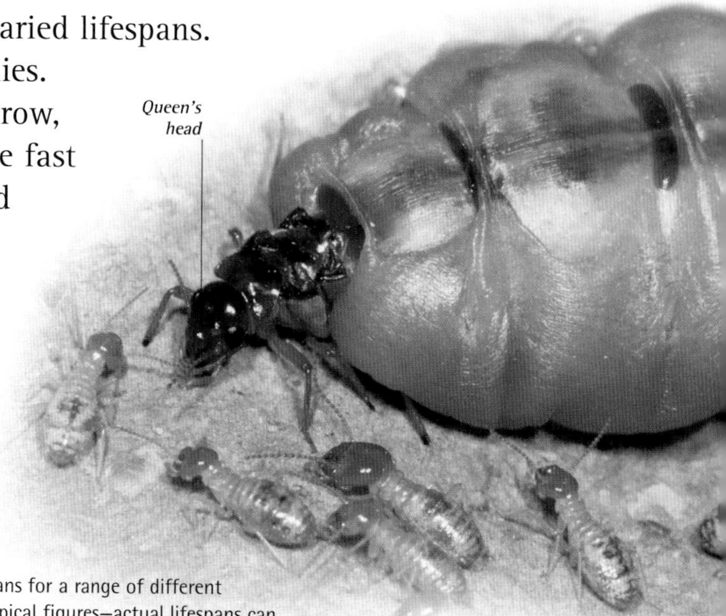

Queen's head

CHALCID WASP: 2 WEEKS

HOUSE FLY: 4 WEEKS

WORKER HONEY BEE: 6 WEEKS

SWALLOWTAIL: 6 MONTHS

DRAGONFLY: 3 YEARS

LONGHORN BEETLE: 10 YEARS

QUEEN TERMITE: 50 YEARS

◀ FAST AND SLOW
This chart shows lifespans for a range of different insects. The ages are typical figures—actual lifespans can vary greatly according to an insect's food supply, the weather, and the time of year. For example, butterflies that start life in spring often die before the summer is over. If the same butterfly starts life in summer, it may spend the winter in hibernation, stretching its lifespan by many months. Some insects can also go into suspended animation if they run out of food or get hit by drought.

▲ LONG LIVE THE QUEEN
Surrounded by attentive workers, this queen termite can look forward to a lengthy but uneventful life. As long as her nest is not attacked by predators, she could survive for many decades, producing thousands of eggs a day. Worker termites provide all her food, and they also keep her body clean, to prevent any infections from setting in. Other social insects also have long-lived queens. Queen wasps and bumble bees rarely survive for more than a year, but queen ants can survive for over 25 years.

Adult mayfly preparing for its final flight

◀ LOPSIDED LIVES
As the sun sets over rivers and lakes in the spring, swarms of mayflies emerge from the water to breed. For mayflies, being adult is a brief experience, because they do not have working mouths or digestive systems, so cannot feed. Their sole task is to mate and scatter their eggs, and so they usually survive as adults for less than one day. However, once the eggs hatch, the young mayflies—called nymphs—have an underwater life spanning from two to three years.

Enormous abdomen
houses the queen's
reproductive system

survival

Adult flies lay
their eggs on fruit

Workers carry
away eggs as soon
as they are laid

▲ SLOWING DOWN AND SPEEDING UP

Unlike us, insects slow down when it is cold and speed up when it is hot. When the temperature is a bracing 50°F (10°C), this fruit fly could live for up to four months, but when it is 85°F (30°C), it can speed through life in just 10 days. In warm conditions, fruit flies—and many other insects—can fit several generations into a single year. Some insects have different generations that fit in with the seasons. For example, aphids often have wingless adults in spring, followed by winged adults later in the year. The wingless adults breed, while the winged ones help the species to spread.

85°F
50°F

Adults crawl up
trees and bushes
after shedding
their skin for a
final time

◄ LIVING IN STEP

After many years spent feeding on nutrient-poor root sap underground, these cicadas have finally turned into adults and are climbing up a tree to mate. In some species, adults emerge every year. But in many, the adults emerge together during "cicada years." In North America, one species stays hidden for exactly 13 years. Every thirteenth year, all the cicadas crawl to the surface and sing to attract mates. Thirteen years later, their offspring do the same thing.

SURVIVING EXTREMES

Without clothes, heating, and air conditioning, humans find it difficult to cope with extremes of hot and cold. We have even more trouble if we cannot get enough oxygen, or if water supplies run low. But for many insects, extremes like these are not a problem. Insects can live in some of the toughest habitats on Earth. They can grow in scalding hot springs, and scuttle across desert sand that would burn human feet. They can survive the freezing conditions of Arctic winters, and the toxic conditions in stagnant pools. Some even spend their entire lives without ever having a drop of water to drink.

survival

HEAT-TOLERANT FLIES ▶
Most insects thrive in warm temperatures, but even they start to flag when the thermometer climbs above 105°F (40°C). But for these flies, 105°F (40°C) is comfortably warm. The flies live around the edges of hot springs, and they lay their eggs on slimy mats of bacteria, which thrive in hot water. The flies run over the surface of the mats, and they can even dive beneath the surface, protected from the heat by wraparound bubbles of air. In winter, the flies stay close to the water, because they die quickly if they get cold.

Fly walking on bacterial mat

▲ HOT HABITATS
This hot spring in Yellowstone National Park is home to heat-tolerant flies. The center of the spring is much too hot for any insect—instead, the flies cluster around the edge, in places where the water is at 110°F (43°C) or below. The world's most heat-tolerant insects are desert-dwelling ants. Some of them forage for food when the surface temperature is above 122°F (50°C). At these temperatures, an egg broken on the ground would slowly cook.

Flies live in narrow zone where the water is relatively cool

Bacterial mats grow around the edge of the spring

STAGNANT WATER

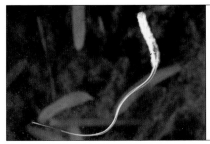

RAT-TAILED MAGGOT
Stagnant water contains little oxygen, but it often has sulfurous compounds that give it a nasty smell. For most animals, it is a dangerous combination, but rat-tailed maggots thrive. Each maggot has a long tube at the end of its body. The tube works like a snorkel, so that it can get oxygen from the air above.

BLOOD WORMS
These wormlike animals are midge larvae, specially adapted for life in stagnant water. They get their red color from hemoglobin, the same substance that is found in human blood. Hemoglobin is good at collecting and carrying oxygen, so the larvae can live in polluted water, where few other animals can survive.

Wax-covered exoskeleton stops water from being lost from the beetle's body

Milled grain contains water that is released when it is digested

▲ LIFE WITHOUT WATER
For us, liquid water is vital—without it, we cannot survive. But many insects, including this flour beetle, live for months or years in habitats that are completely dry. Flour beetles eat cereals, flour, and milled grain, and they get all the water they need from their food. In deserts, insects often use different techniques to survive. One kind of beetle, from the Namib Desert in southwest Africa, climbs up dunes on foggy nights and collects drops of water that condense on its body.

Frost-covered wings

▲ INSECT ANTIFREEZE
After a frosty night in early fall, this black darter dragonfly is covered with frost at sunrise. The frost will not do any permanent damage to the dragonfly because it is only on the outside. The inside of the dragonfly's body is protected by an antifreeze similar to the one used in cars. On mountains, and in the Arctic, many insects depend on this antifreeze to survive. Some can survive temperatures below -75°F (-60°C)—far colder than a deep freeze.

SHUTTING DOWN

With its wings tucked underneath its body, this queen wasp is sleeping through the winter. She goes into a suspended animation and will reawaken when the weather is warmer. Many other insects also hibernate, either as eggs, larvae, pupae, or adults. Insects can also become dormant in extreme heat and during extended droughts.

When some insects shut down, their bodies lose most of their water, and their chemistry comes to a halt. In this state, one kind of midge larva can survive being dipped in liquid helium, at a temperature of -454°F (-270°C)—the same as outer space. When the larva is warmed up and moistened, it miraculously comes back to life.

SOCIAL INSECTS

Most insects live on their own, and leave their young to look after themselves. Social insects are very different because they live in colonies or permanent family groups. Some colonies contain only a few dozen members, but the biggest can have many millions. The insects in a colony work as a team, building a nest, finding food, and raising the colony's young. Social insects include all ants and termites, and many species of bees and wasps. By living and working together, they have become some of the most successful animals on Earth.

WORKER

Hair-fringed pollen baskets on hindlegs

DRONE

Large eyes

Extra-large abdomen

QUEEN

HONEY BEES AT HOME ▶
These worker bees are clustered on a honeycomb, deep inside their nest. The honeycomb is made of wax, and it is like a hanging storage system, full of six-sided cells. Some of the cells contain honey, which the bees have made by gathering nectar from flowers and bringing it back to the nest. Other cells contain young bees that are growing up, or new eggs that have been laid by the queen. The enlarged picture on the right shows cells that have larvae curled up inside them.

Young larva curled up in an open cell

◀ HONEY BEE CASTES
In a honey bee nest, there are three castes (types) of bee. Worker bees are the most numerous. They are sterile females (they cannot reproduce), and they build the nest, maintain it, and raise the young. Drones are male bees that mate with new queens to start new nests. The queen rules the nest by producing a chemical that suppresses (stops) the reproductive system of the workers, so that only the queen bee lays eggs.

50–250 ADULTS PER COLONY	100–500 ADULTS PER COLONY	25,000–1 MILLION ADULTS PER COLONY

▲ PAPER WASPS
These wasps make nests from wood fibers, which they chew up to make paper. They hang their nests in the open, usually on plant stems. Their colonies can be small, with as few as 50 adults.

▲ BUMBLE BEES
Bumble bees often breed in the warmth of old mouse nests. In the spring, nests contain only a dozen workers, together with the queen. By late summer, the number of workers can rise to 500. Bumble bees raise their larvae in oval cells made from yellow wax.

▲ WOOD ANTS
These ants are swarming out of their nest after hibernation. They make their nests from pine needles and small twigs in the spring, and raise their young in tunnels beneath the surface.

HONEYCOMB KEY

1. **Worker bee:** Workers carry out the maintenance tasks in the nest. They also collect food, make honey, and feed developing larvae.

2. **Larva:** Cells containing larvae are left open, so that the worker bees can feed them.

3. **Meeting and greeting:** Workers communicate by touching each other with their antennae and by carrying out special dances.

4. **Honey storage:** Cells containing honey are sealed with caps of white wax. Bees use honey as their winter food.

5. **Empty cell:** Workers make cells with wax from their bodies. The cells are six-sided, so fit together without any wasted space.

6. **Egg:** The queen bee lays eggs in the cells. In commercial hives, she is kept away from the cells so that they just contain honey.

7. **Pupa:** While a larva pupates, its cell is covered by a yellow waxy cap. In about 12 days the pupa emerges.

e▸▸ social insects

| 50,000–75,000 ADULTS PER COLONY | UP TO 5 MILLION ADULTS PER COLONY | UP TO 20 MILLION ADULTS PER COLONY |

▲ HONEY BEES
The nests of honey bees last several years. In the spring and summer, the number of bees grows because there is plenty of food. The queen and workers hibernate in the fall and winter.

▲ TERMITES
The colonies of termites vary in size. Some live in nests a few inches across, while others build structures many feet high. Termites rarely feed in the open—they chew through wood from the inside, crossing open spaces in tunnels made of mud.

▲ DRIVER ANTS
These ants are nomadic—they make temporary nests at night by linking their legs together. They feed on small animals and insects, swarming and overpowering their prey.

BEES, WASPS, AND ANTS

This group contains some of the world's most successful insects, as well as some that have a powerful sting. Although they look different, bees, wasps, and ants are close relatives. Most of them—aside from some ants—have two pairs of wings and a slender waist. Solitary species live on their own, but social species live in giant families called colonies and raise their young in nests. Bees feed on pollen and nectar, but wasps and ants eat a wide range of food. Many species play an important role in pollinating plants or controlling pests.

bees, wasps, and ants

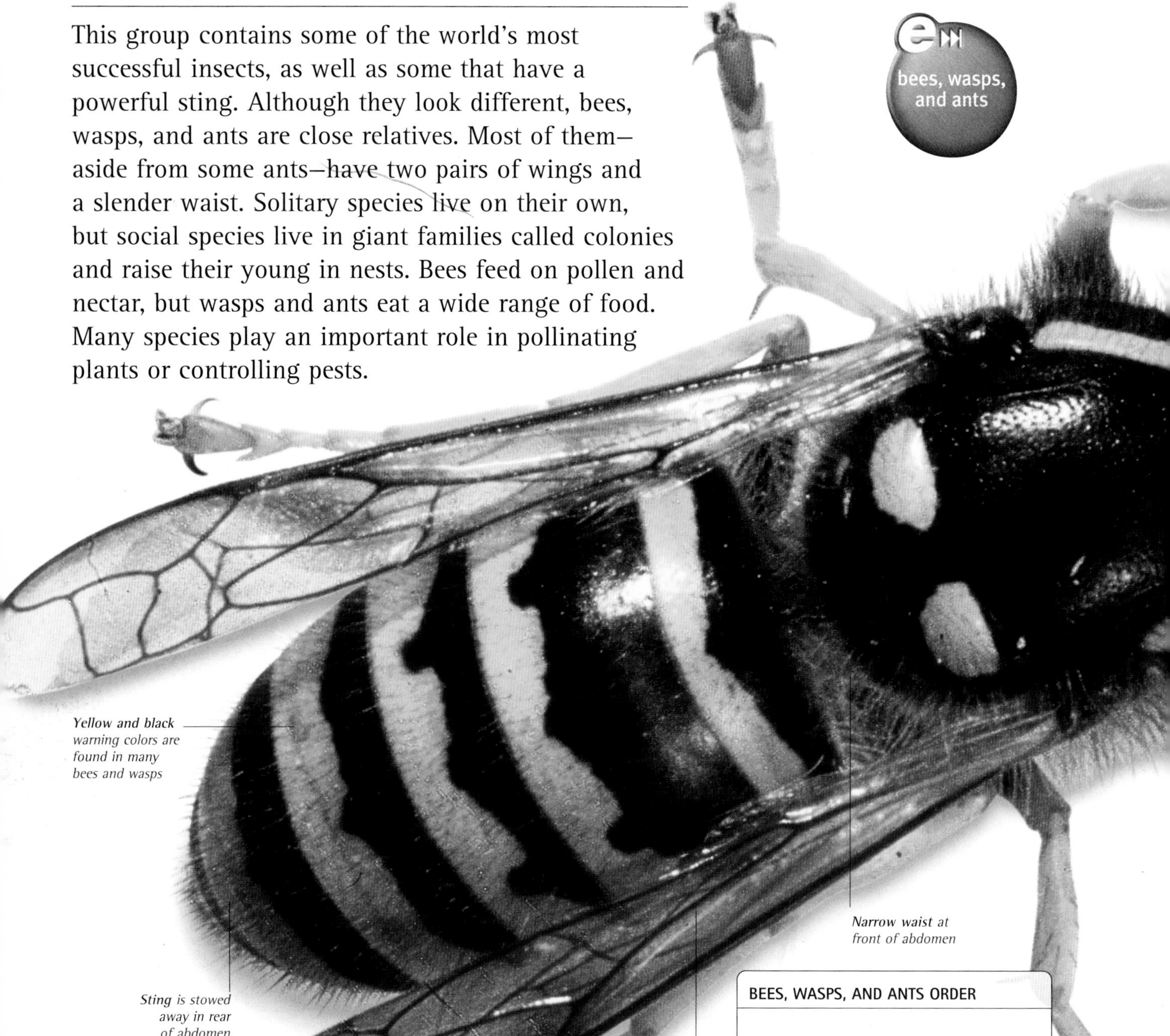

Yellow and black warning colors are found in many bees and wasps

Narrow waist at front of abdomen

Sting is stowed away in rear of abdomen

Hind wings are much smaller than the forewings

Hooked claws for carrying caterpillars and other insects

WARNING STRIPES ▲

With its bold black and yellow markings, this common wasp advertises the fact that it can sting. Like most bees and wasps, it has slender wings that fold away along its sides. Its forewings and hind wings link up with tiny hooks and beat together when it flies. Wasps have large eyes, thick antennae, and biting mouthparts. The adults eat fruit and other sugary foods, but they feed their larvae on insects, chewed into a nutritious pulp.

BEES, WASPS, AND ANTS ORDER

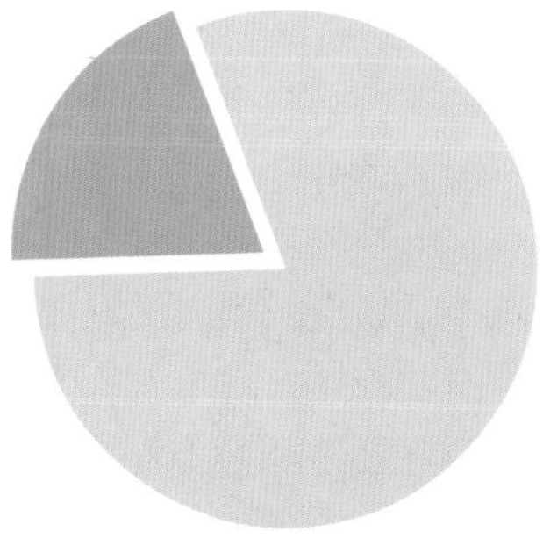

Bees, wasps, and ants make up the order Hymenoptera, which contains 200,000 species—20 percent of known insect species. Bees and wasps include both solitary and social species. Ants always live in groups and are probably the most numerous insects on Earth.

DEVELOPMENT OF A HONEY BEE

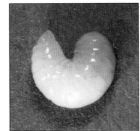

EGG
Bees develop by complete metamorphosis, which means that they change shape completely as they grow. In a honey bee hive, only the queen lays eggs. In summer, she can produce more than 2,000 eggs a day, gluing each one to the bottom of an empty cell. Four days later, the egg hatches to produce a larva.

LARVA
Honey bee larvae are white and do not have any legs. They are fed by young workers in the hive known as nurse bees, who give them a mixture of honey and pollen. This is called bee bread. Larvae grow quickly on this rich diet. About six days after hatching, a larva is fully grown and ready to turn into a pupa.

PUPA
The larva turns into a pupa by shedding its skin and spinning a cocoon. Meanwhile, the nurse bees seal it in the cell by making a wax lid. During the next 10 to 12 days, the larva's body is broken down, and an adult body is assembled in its place. Three weeks after the egg was laid, an adult worker bee crawls out.

ADULT WORKER
Worker bees live for about six weeks. During that time their work depends upon their age. In their first week, they act as nurse bees, feeding the next wave of larvae. During the next week, they maintain the hive and make their first flights. Finally, they become foragers, collecting nectar and pollen from flowers.

Sensitive antennae are segmented for flexibility

Antennae have a sharp bend

Thorax in worker ants is often longer than the abdomen

Large compound eyes used for finding insect prey

Three simple eyes (ocelli) on top of the head

WORKERS WITHOUT WINGS ►
Worker ants often have stings, but they do not have wings. Compared to bees and wasps, they have a long thorax but a short abdomen, which gives them a stretched-out look. Worker ants have small eyes but well-developed antennae, and they find their way mainly by smell. When ants breed, their nests also contain winged males and females. These flying ants leave the nest in summer to start nests of their own.

Smaller workers climb aboard the pieces of leaf to ward off predatory flies

Large workers carry the leaves back to the nest

Strong legs with hooked claws for gripping

▲ DIFFERENT DIETS
These leafcutter ants have cut out some pieces of leaf and are carrying them back to their underground nest. Instead of feeding on the leaves right away, they pile them up in a compost heap. A special fungus grows on the heap, and the ants use this as food. Compared to leafcutters, most ants have more varied diets. Many eat seeds, fruit, and anything sweet. Some catch insects and other small animals, killing them with their stings.

▲ PARASITES AND HOSTS
Drilling into a tree trunk, this female wood wasp or horntail is about to lay an egg. Her larva will tunnel through the tree, eating rotting wood and fungi. However, as the larva feeds, it risks attack by a parasitic ichneumon wasp. The ichneumon senses the grub and drills down through the wood to lay her egg in the grub. The ichneumon wasps may seem gruesome, but they do useful work by keeping pests such as the wood wasp under control.

INSECT ARCHITECTS

Despite their small size, insects include some of the most skillful builders in the animal world. They work by instinct, instead of planning ahead, and they use a wide range of building materials. Some insect builders work on their own, but the biggest structures are made by social species, which work together as a team. Termites make the largest nests—some tropical species build immense mounds up to 23 ft (7 m) high. These nests are even bigger than they look, because part of their structure is hidden underground.

TERMITE TOWER ►
This towering termite nest weighs more than a ton. It is built from damp clay that has slowly baked hard in the tropical sunshine. The termites moisten the clay with their saliva, building it up into pillars with supports that give the nest its strength. During the daytime, the nest appears to be abandoned, because termites spend the daylight hours inside. When night falls, the workers forage for pieces of dead plants outside the nest.

Tower above the underground nest

Air channel leading up to tower

insect homes

Plant remains collected by workers

Fungus growing in fungus gardens

Brood chambers containing eggs an developing termites

Royal chamber containing the king and queen

◄ INSIDE THE NEST
In this African termite nest, the tower works as an air conditioner, keeping the nest moist and cool. The main feeding and breeding quarters are in a dome close to the ground. Here, the worker termites collect their own droppings and use them to grow a special fungus, which is the termites' main food. Below these fungus gardens is the royal chamber, where the queen lays her eggs, and the brood chambers, where the eggs hatch and develop.

◄ BUILDING WITH PAPER

Long before humans invented paper, insects were using it to build their nests. This wasp nest is made from several layers of paper, built around a multilayered comb. Paper is a good insulator, so it keeps the developing grubs warm. Wasps make paper by chewing up wood fibers, and then spreading the pulp out in sheets. As the summer progresses, they tear down the inner walls and make new outer ones, so that the nest can expand.

Section cut away to show brood combs inside

Worker wasp feeds larvae on chewed-up insects

Sealed cells containing developing pupae

Paper traps air, making it good at retaining heat

Nest is made of several overlapping layers

Narrow entrance faces downward, keeping warm air inside

Scraped-up wood fibers are used to make paper

▲ MAKING PAPER

Using its jaws, this worker wasp is scraping up wood fibers to carry back to its nest. It will mix the fibers with saliva, before spreading them out in a papery sheet. The color of the nest depends on the type of wood used. Wood-eating termites make a similar building material, known as carton. Some species use carton to make round nests, as big as soccer balls, high up in trees.

SOLITARY BUILDERS ►

Building a nest does not always involve teamwork. This female potter wasp has made a flask-shaped nest from mud, and is stocking it with a caterpillar that she has paralyzed with her sting. She will lay an egg beside it, and then seal the nest. When the egg hatches, the young larva will feed on the caterpillar, before turning into a adult wasp and flying away. Potter wasps are common in warm parts of the world.

Wasp drags caterpillar to the nest

MOBILE HOMES

LEAFY LODGINGS
Most insect architects build homes to raise their young, but a few make homes to protect themselves. This caddisfly larva lives in streams and protects itself by making a case of leaves. The larva keeps most of its body inside the case, but reaches outward to collect its food. As it grows, it adds more leaves to the case.

PRECISION BUILDING
Different species of caddisfly make different cases with their own building techniques. This larva makes its case out of leaves and plant stems, cutting them up into same-sized pieces. It arranges them in a spiral, fastened together with silk. The result is a neat tube, up to 2 in (5 cm) long and about as thick as a pencil.

SAFETY AMONG STONES
This species of caddisfly has fast-moving larvae that do not build cases. When the larva turns into a pupa though, it needs to protect itself from predators. It does this by spinning a shroud of silk, with small stones attached to it. The pupa and its shroud are attached to a rock, making it hard for predators to eat.

REACHING OUT
Caddisfly larvae have soft abdomens, which they usually keep stowed inside their cases. This one has reached out to look for food. This species starts its case by making a small basket from tiny pieces of root. As it grows, it adds chopped-up plant stems, fastened together with the silk made by all caddisflies.

LIFE IN A GROUP

When honey bees are looking for food, they work as a well-organized team. If one bee finds a good place for flowers, it flies back to the nest and spreads the news. Using a special dance, it tells its fellow workers where the food is, and also how far they have to travel to reach it. It is an astonishing system, and it makes honey bees some of the most efficient food-finders on Earth. Like honey bees, all other social insects show special kinds of group behavior. By passing on information, and by sharing out different tasks, they have the best chance of success.

SUN

ANGLE

FOOD

WAGGLE

NEST

◄ WAGGLE DANCE
Worker bees use two different dances to guide their nest-mates toward food. The round dance shows that food is nearby. The faster the dance, the more food there is. The waggle dance, shown here, is used when the food is farther away. The bee moves in a figure-eight, waggling as it crosses the middle. The speed of the dance shows how far away the flowers are. The angle of the waggle shows the direction of the flowers in relation to the Sun.

▼ KEEPING IN TOUCH
These ants have met on a trail and are communicating by smell. To keep in touch, they pass on chemical messages by releasing substances into the environment called pheromones. Workers use pheromones to mark food trails, and to raise the alarm if they are attacked. In the heart of the nest, the queen gives off her own pheromones to keep the colony running smoothly. If the queen dies, her pheromone production stops, and another queen steps in to take her place.

Antennae detect pheromones and the scent of food

Glands in the ant's abdomen leave a trail of scent

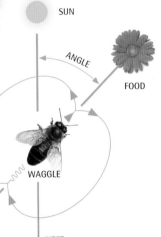

▲ STOWAWAYS IN THE NEST

Like any communication system, pheromones can be misused. This caterpillar, of a butterfly called an alcon blue, mimics an ant pupa by copying its pheromones and its shape. Worker ants mistake it for a pupa and carry it into their nest. Once the caterpillar is underground, it turns into a voracious predator, feeding on the ants' eggs and grubs. Many other insects use similar tricks. Some feed on their hosts, but others simply use the nest as a home.

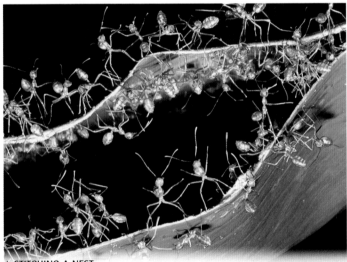

▲ STITCHING A NEST

Weaver ants make nests by folding leaves in half and then sticking them together with silk. These worker ants have started the task, folding over a leaf so that its edges almost touch. Next, the workers bridge the gap with their legs, and slowly pull the two edges together. Finally comes the silk, which is produced by the ant larvae. Workers pick up the larvae in their jaws and then dab the sticky silk across the gap. Once the silk has hardened, the join is complete.

social insects

DAILY TASKS

FEEDING THE YOUNG

In any insect nest, feeding the young is a vital task. These paper wasps have arrived at their nest with food, which they will give to larvae in their cells. Growing larvae usually receive small meals at frequent intervals. For example, a honey bee larva is fed about 150 times in six days while it develops into a pupa. Bee and wasp larvae cannot collect food themselves, so they rely on being fed on time.

CLIMATE CONTROL

In a honey bee hive, worker bees control the temperature of the nest. These workers are fanning their wings to blow cool air into a hive. This job is important in summer, because honey bee larvae die if the temperature rises above 97°F (36°C). If the nest is in danger of overheating, the workers take emergency action by spreading drops of water over the cells to cool them.

NEST REPAIRS

If an insect nest is damaged, workers make repairs. These termites are sealing a hole in their nest, using supplies of fresh mud. Within a few days, the repair will harden, and the breach will be sealed. If the damage affects the breeding quarters, workers quickly gather around the larvae or pupae and carry them to safety. Once they are off the scene, repairs can get under way.

DISPOSING OF THE DEAD

In a large nest, dozens of workers die every day. To prevent disease, it is important that their bodies be cleared away. This ant will dispose of the corpse once it is far enough from the nest. In honey bee nests, this kind of work becomes important in the fall when lots of workers die. The survivors cluster together in the middle of the nest, waiting for warmer times in spring.

NEST DEFENSE

These wood ants are spraying formic acid into the air to defend their nest from attack. Social insects react quickly to danger, releasing pheromones that call other workers to their aid. Ants and termites have special soldier castes, which keep constant guard against invaders. Many have large jaws, but soldier termites, called nasutes, have heads like nozzles and squirt out a sticky glue.

SWARMS

Swarms are a spectacular and sometimes scary feature of insect life. Without any warning, millions of scuttling, rustling insects can suddenly appear. When the insects are locusts, and they land to feed on farmers' crops, the result can be disastrous, leaving many people short of food. Swarming insects can also be dangerous, particularly if they have powerful stings. Many swarms are formed by social insects, such as ants or bees, but some of the most common swarms contain insects that normally lead individual lives.

▼ LOCUSTS ON THE MOVE

These desert locusts are searching for food, while local people try to drive them away. Locusts usually live on their own, but swarm after moist weather lets them raise lots of young, causing overcrowding and food shortages. Locusts are a serious problem in Africa and other warm parts of the world. The largest locust swarm ever recorded came from North America. It contained more than 10 trillion insects and weighed more than 25 million tons.

▲ RAIDING PARTY

Unlike locusts, ants live in swarms for the whole of their lives. After camping in a bivouac (temporary shelter) overnight, these predatory army ants are setting off in search of their prey. At first, the ants march in a long column, but they soon start to fan out to 50 ft (15 m) wide. With so many ants on the move, insects and other ground-dwelling animals find it difficult to escape.

Local people try to save their crops from being eaten

▲ BEE SWARMS

These worker honey bees have formed a swarm hanging from a tree branch. Somewhere inside the swarm is a young queen bee, who is ready to start a new nest. While the swarm clusters around the queen, scout bees set off to search for nest sites. When a good site has been found, the swarm moves off and settles in. Honey bee swarms often look dangerous, but swarming bees are usually good-tempered, and rarely sting.

▲ SWARMING ON THE SPOT

On still days in spring, male midges, or gnats, often gather in swarms and hang in the air like clouds of smoke. Gnats normally live on their own, but, during the breeding season, the males gather together to attract females. If a female approaches the cloud, a male quickly approaches her, and the two insects fly away. Unlike many swarms, this kind can last for less than an hour. If the weather changes and a breeze starts blowing, the swarm quickly breaks up.

e ▸▸

swarms

PREYING ON SWARMS ▶

Swarming is useful for midges because it helps males and females to find each other. But the swarms also attract biting midges—like the one shown here. Instead of joining the swarm, they prey on the swarmers themselves. Swarms of insects also attract other predators, such as birds. Many birds are fond of flying ants, and they snap them up as they pour out of their nests and into the sky.

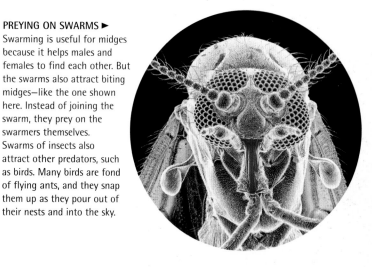

Swarming locusts search for food

SHELTERING IN A SWARM

These ladybugs have gathered together to hibernate. This is a swarm with a difference, because it barely moves. The ladybugs stay together throughout cold weather and go their separate ways in the spring. Flies also form hibernation swarms. One European species, called the cluster fly, often swarms in empty rooms and attics if it gets a chance to fly indoors. Some of the biggest hibernation swarms are formed by butterflies and moths.

MIGRATION

Insects are some of the greatest travelers in the natural world. Every year, billions of butterflies fly huge distances to reach the places where they breed. Once they have bred, they and their young head back to their winter homes. But butterflies are not alone. All kinds of insects—including dragonflies, grasshoppers, moths, and thrips—make seasonal journeys as well. Insects rely entirely on their own muscles to take them where they want to go, and they are guided by instinct, which tells them where to go. Their journeys are called migrations. By migrating, insects make the most of different conditions in different parts of the world.

▲ READY TO GO
Perched on lakeside reeds, these dragonflies are about to start a long flight southward, from Mongolia toward southern Asia. The journey is risky, because they can be hit by sudden storms or attacked by predators such as birds. Many will die on the outward journey, and more will die on the way back. But for the survivors, migration has one big advantage—they can avoid the freezing Mongolian winter.

migration

◄ BLOWN IN THE WIND
Small migrants—such as this sap-sucking thrip—are not strong fliers, but they can travel a long way with help from the wind. In summer, they are sometimes sucked high into the air by thunderstorms. After being blown along in a storm, they slowly drift back toward the ground. When insects migrate like this, they cannot steer, but if luck is on their side, they land in places where there is plenty of food.

Slender and hair-fringed wings

◀ WINTER GATHERING

Clustered on the trunk of a pine tree, these monarch butterflies have reached their winter home in Mexico. For several months, the butterflies will remain on the tree, taking short flights when the weather is mild. In spring, when the temperatures warm up, they will set off on a northward journey toward their distant breeding grounds. Not all monarchs join these winter gatherings. Some stay where they grew up, hibernating in hollow trees or under bark.

Monarchs cluster together on the sunlit side of pine trees

Butterflies bask with their wings open on sunny days

MONARCH MIGRATION PATH

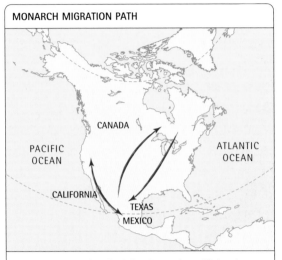

CANADA

PACIFIC OCEAN

ATLANTIC OCEAN

CALIFORNIA

TEXAS

MEXICO

Monarch butterflies from North America are the world's best-known insect travelers. Most of them spend the winter in the south of the continent—either in California, or in an area that includes Texas and northern Mexico. In the spring and summer some monarchs travel as far as Canada—a distance of 1,860 miles (3,000 km).

The butterflies that fly northwards in summer often breed and then die before the journey is finished. Their young then complete the northward leg, before flying south when summer comes to an end.

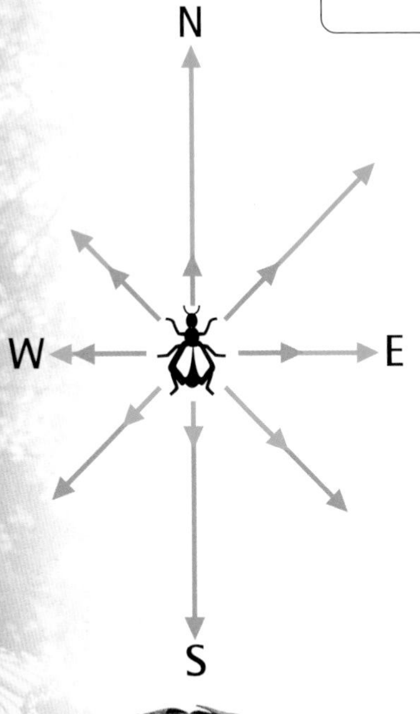

N

W

E

S

◀ KEEPING ON COURSE

This diagram shows how much time a typical insect spends flying in different directions as it migrates. In spring, its overall direction is northward, although it flies in other directions as well. In the fall, things are reversed, and the overall direction is south. If the insect lives in the southern hemisphere, rather than the northern one, the pattern would be the other way around. Insects steer by using an onboard compass, but they also follow landmarks, such as coasts.

SPRING

FALL

Locust mummified in ice

▲ LOST IN TRANSIT

Eight hundred years ago, this locust crash-landed on Knifepoint Glacier, in Wyoming. Scientists discovered its remains when they investigated the glacier's ice. This locust—and many others like it—died during migration. Bad luck can strike migrants in many ways. Ships sometimes sail through clouds of butterflies that have lost their way. Once insects are over the open ocean, they have a slim chance of making it back to land.

INSECTS AND PEOPLE

Many people have mixed feelings about insects—particularly those that bite and sting, or ones that find their way indoors. Insects can be a nuisance, but some cause much more serious problems by feeding on crops, or by spreading disease. But some insects can be helpful. They provide us with useful products, such as silk and honey, and they perform an extremely important service by pollinating many of the world's plants. Without them, the living world would be a different and much less interesting place.

insects and people

Smoke encourages bees to stop flying and settle on the combs

Beekeepers wear protective clothing

Thread is wound around a wooden bobbin

Several strands join together to make a thread

Cocoons float in a pan of warm water

Honeycomb inside wooden frame

▲ MAKING SILK

Commercial silk is made by silkworms—the caterpillars of a flightless moth. When the caterpillars pupate, they wrap themselves in thick silk cocoons. Here, silk is being unwound in the traditional way, by floating the cocoons in water. Each cocoon can produce a strand of silk up to 3,000 ft (900 m) long. Silkmoths were first bred in China, over 4,500 years ago. Today, they no longer live in the wild.

◄ COLLECTING HONEY

Dressed from head to toe in a bee-proof suit, this beekeeper has opened up a hive to remove some of its honeycombs. At his side is a smoke gun, which he puffs over the bees to keep them under control. The bees build their honeycombs inside square wooden frames. The beekeeper lifts these out, scrapes the wax lids off the cells, and then spins the frames in a centrifuge (rotating machine that separates liquids). This forces the honey out of the cells.

Frames are stacked vertically inside the hive

▲ COLORADO BEETLE
Colorado beetles chew their way through potato leaves. These insect pests originally came from North America, but since the 1850s they have been accidentally carried to many other parts of the world. Each female can lay up to 3,000 eggs a year, and the beetles can produce three generations a year. They can devastate fields of potatoes unless they are brought under control.

▲ GYPSY MOTH
This small white moth originally comes from Europe and Asia, where its caterpillars feed on the leaves of trees. In the 1860s, it was deliberately taken to North America in an attempt to raise its caterpillars for silk. However, the adult moths escaped into nearby woodlands, and soon began to spread. In North America, gypsy moths have few natural enemies, so their caterpillars can completely strip trees of their leaves. Today, gypsy moths are still spreading, and forests have to be sprayed when severe outbreaks occur.

▲ MEDITERRANEAN FRUIT FLY
This destructive pest lays its eggs on all kinds of fruit. Its larvae eat their way through the fruit, leaving it unfit for sale. Originally from Africa, this fruit fly has spread to most warm parts of the world. Because this little fly causes so much damage, great efforts are taken to keep it out of fruit-growing regions. Many parts of the world have special quarantine regulations to keep it at bay.

▲ MOBILE HIVES
Most beehives stay in one place, but this truck is loaded with beehives that spend the spring and summer on the move. The hives are rented out to fruit farmers and then collected a few weeks later when the task of pollination is done. Honey bees adapt surprisingly well to this traveling lifestyle. Each time they move, they quickly get their bearings, so they can find their way back to their own hive.

◄ INSECTS AS FOOD
Roasted and spread on a tortilla, grasshoppers make a nutritious and crunchy meal. This insect-based recipe comes from Mexico, but insects are also eaten in many other parts of the world. Insects contain lots of protein, but only small amounts of fat. In the Western world, many people find the idea of eating insects off-putting, even though they happily eat animals related to insects, such as lobsters, shrimps, and crabs.

HOW MOSQUITOES SPREAD MALARIA

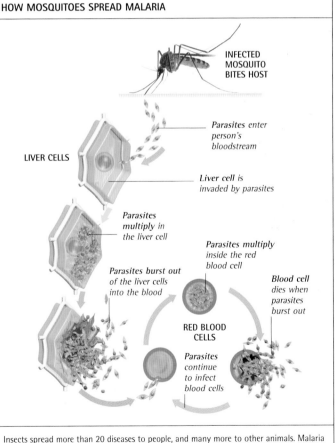

Insects spread more than 20 diseases to people, and many more to other animals. Malaria is one of the most dangerous, affecting several million people every year. The disease is caused by a single-celled parasite, which lives in mosquitoes' salivary glands. When an infected mosquito bites a human host, the parasite enters the person's bloodstream and infects their liver cells. Here they multiply, and then pour back into the blood, where they multiply again. Malaria causes severe fever, and sometimes fatal damage to the kidneys and brain. The mosquitoes pick up the disease by biting people who are already infected.

STUDYING INSECTS

Insect specialists are known as entomologists. They study insects to see how they live, and to find out how they affect us and the rest of the living world. Thanks to their research, a great deal is known about useful insects, and about those that attack crops or cause disease. Entomologists also study the way we affect insects, when we alter or damage the natural world. However, other scientists study them too. For example, geneticists have made important discoveries about genes and inheritance by studying tiny flies. Insects have also inspired engineers, giving them ideas for six-legged robots, and even miniature planes.

▲ FLIES IN FOCUS

Lined up in plastic cells, these fruit flies are about to go under the microscope so their features can be studied. For geneticists, these little flies are extremely useful animals, because they are easy to raise and breed very quickly. Fruit flies also have another plus. Although they are small, their bodies contain extra-large chromosomes—the threads of DNA that carry an animal's genes. This helps scientists to investigate the way chromosomes work.

One microprocessor controls each leg

Electric servo motors power each leg

On-board battery pack provides power

INSPIRED BY INSECTS ▶
Attila is a robot insect that has been developed at the Massachusetts Institute of Technology (MIT). Measuring 12 in (30 cm) long, and weighing just over 3 lbs (1.5 kg), it has 23 separate motors that control its six legs. Atilla moves like an insect and can clamber over rough terrain all by itself, using cameras and microprocessors to steer its way. In the future, machines like this might explore the surface of distant planets, such as Mars.

Robot always keeps at least three legs on the ground at once

One or two legs move at any one time

Electronic programming in the microprocessors stop the leg pushing if it threatens to tip the robot over

Twin cameras swivel to inspect the terrain

Openings at the top to let out the odor

Pieces of cardboard inside the trap release fake pheromone

▲ TRAPPED BY SCENT

This plastic trap is designed to catch boll weevils, which are pests in cotton fields. The trap releases a substance that mimics one of the weevil's pheromones. In the wild, boll weevils use the pheromone to attract each other. When they smell the fake pheromone, they clamber into the trap and get caught. Traps like this are used against many insect pests. Unlike pesticides, they eliminate harmful insects without killing helpful ones.

INSECT ALLIES ►

During the 1920s, a prickly pear cactus plague threatened vast areas of Australian farmland. To fight its spread, entomologists brought in an Argentinian cactus-eating moth. They reared the moths in captivity and scattered three billion eggs on the wild cacti. Within 10 years, the plague was over. Today, the moth still keeps the cactus under control.

e ►► insects and people

Legs can swing vertically and horizontally

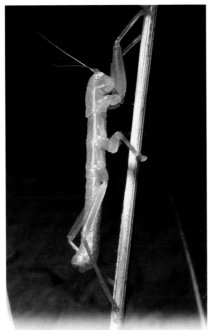

▲ DISCOVERING NEW SPECIES

In 2002, entomologists discovered this extraordinary insect in the mountains of Namibia. New insects are found all the time, but this one was particularly exciting, because nothing like it had ever been seen before. After studying it, scientists decided to call it a mantophasmid, which means "part mantis, part stick-insect." Since then, several other mantophasmids have been discovered.

INSECTS UNDER THREAT

DRAGONFLIES AND DAMSELFLIES

All over the world, insects are threatened by the changes that humans make to the natural world. For dragonflies and damselflies, the main threat is drainage of freshwater wetlands, including marshes and ponds. This San Francisco damselfly lives in a busy part of California, which puts it particularly at risk.

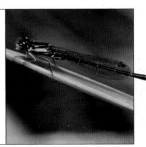

BEETLES

Beetle larvae feed on living trees or on dead wood. This means that beetles are harmed when forests are cut down and dead trees are cleared away. Wood-boring beetles develop slowly, so it takes them a long time to recover. This splendor beetle is a wood-borer, and is now one of the rarest insects in Europe.

BUTTERFLIES

The Queen Alexandra's birdwing butterfly is captured by collectors because it is one of the largest butterflies in the world. Like all insects, butterflies are also threatened by the world's rapidly changing climate. Entomologists are studying butterflies closely to see what effect this has.

INSECT CLASSIFICATION

Subclass APTERYGOTA *Primitive wingless insects*

Order	Common Name	Families	Species	Distribution	Key Features
Archaeognatha	Bristletail	2	350	Worldwide	Wingless insects with humpbacked bodies, compound eyes, and three tails resembling fine bristles. They often live in crevices and move by crawling or jumping.
Thysanura	Silverfish	4	370	Worldwide	Wingless insects with slender bodies and three abdominal tails. The body is often covered with silvery scales, giving a fishlike appearance. Often found in decaying plant matter, and indoors.

Subclass PTERYGOTA *Winged (although some are secondarily wingless) insects*

Division EXOPTERYGOTA *Insects that develop by incomplete metamorphosis*

Ephemeroptera	Mayflies	23	2,500	Worldwide except Antarctica	Long-bodied insects with two pairs of wings. Adults do not feed, and often live for less than a day. Nymphs live in freshwater and feed on plants or on animals.
Odonata	Dragonflies and damselflies	30	5,500	Worldwide except Antarctica	Long-bodied insects with two pairs of wings, a slender abdomen, and prominent compound eyes. Adults feed on other insects, often catching them in midair. Nymphs live in freshwater.
Plecoptera	Stoneflies	15	2,000	Worldwide except Antarctica	Weak-flying insects with flattened bodies and two pairs of filmy wings. Nymphs live in freshwater, molting up to 30 times before becoming adults.
Grylloblattodea	Rock-crawlers	1	25	Asia and North America	Long-bodied wingless insects that live among rocks. They have small heads and eyes, but well-developed legs, and are able to remain active at low temperatures.
Orthoptera	Crickets and grasshoppers	28	20,000	Worldwide except Antarctica	Heavily built insects with chewing mouthparts, toughened forewings, and well-developed hind legs. Most are plant-feeders, but some hunt or scavenge.
Phasmatodea	Stick and leaf insects	3	2,500	Worldwide except polar regions	Slow-moving, plant-eating insects with slender bodies, typically camouflaged to look like twigs or leaves. Females are usually wingless. In some species, females breed without mating, and males are rare or unknown.
Mantophasmatodea	Mantophasmids	1	13	Southern Africa	Carnivorous wingless insects with long bodies, long antennae, and well-developed legs. The order is the most recently recognized, described in 2002.
Mantodea	Praying mantises	8	2,000	Worldwide except polar regions	Long-bodied carnivorous insects that hunt by stealth, using grasping front legs equipped with spines. Mantises have keen eyesight, highly mobile heads, and two pairs of wings. Their wingless nymphs are also predatory.
Dermaptera	Earwigs	10	1,900	Worldwide except polar regions	Insects with long flat bodies ending in a pair of abdominal pincers. Most species are winged with intricately folded hind wings tucked under much shorter forewings. Earwigs eat plant and animal food.
Blattodea	Cockroaches	6	4,000	Worldwide except polar regions	Insects with a flattened oval shape, chewing mouthparts, and well-developed legs. Most species have two pairs of wings.
Embioptera	Web-spinners	8	300	Subtropical and tropical regions	These insects live in silk tunnels, in soil, or in leaf litter. Both sexes have spoon-shaped front legs, containing silk glands. Males are winged, but females are wingless.
Isoptera	Termites	7	2,750	Worldwide in tropical and warm temperate regions	Plant-eating insects that live in large colonies, sometimes in elaborate nests. Workers are wingless, but reproductives have two pairs of wings.
Zoraptera	Angel insects	1	29	Subtropical and tropical regions, except Australia	Small termitelike insects that live in rotting wood and leaf litter. In most species, adults have winged and wingless forms.

Order	Common Name	Families	Species	Distribution	Key Features
Psocoptera	Bark lice and book lice	35	3,000	Worldwide	Small insects that typically live on trees, in leaf litter, or indoors. Most adults are blunt-headed, with two pairs of wings, but book lice are frequently wingless.
Phthiraptera	Parasitic lice	25	6,000	Worldwide	Wingless parasitic insects that live on mammals and birds, feeding on their blood. Each species normally lives on a single type of host.
Hemiptera	True bugs	134	82,000	Worldwide except Antarctica	Diverse insects that feed on plants or animals, using mouthparts that pierce and suck. In winged forms, the forewings are often leathery, protecting the hind wings when they are closed. Bugs live in many habitats.
Thysanoptera	Thrips	8	5,000	Worldwide except Antarctica	Small or minute insects with slender bodies and two pairs of feathery wings. Many species feed on juices from plants, and some are serious pests of crops.

Division ENDOPTERYGOTA *Insects that develop by complete metamorphosis*

Order	Common Name	Families	Species	Distribution	Key Features
Megaloptera	Alder flies and dobson flies	2	300	Worldwide except Antarctica	Waterside insects with two pairs of wings that are similar in shape and in size. Adults do not feed. Their larvae are carnivorous and live in freshwater.
Rhaphidioptera	Snake flies	2	150	Worldwide except Antarctica	Predatory insects with two pairs of wings, chewing mouthparts, and a long neck that lunges forward when attacking prey. Larvae are also predatory.
Neuroptera	Ant lions and lacewings	17	4,000	Worldwide except Antarctica	Predatory insects with two pairs of similarly sized wings, with an intricate network of veins. Larvae have large jaws and are also carnivorous.
Coleoptera	Beetles	166	370,000	Worldwide	Insects with hardened forewings (elytra) that fit over their hind wings like a case. Beetles have a vast range of habitats, lifestyles, and diets. The larvae can be legless, burrowing their way through food.
Strepsiptera	Stylopids	8	560	Worldwide	Small insects that live parasitically on other insects. Males have distinctively twisted hind wings. Females are wingless and spend their lives in their host.
Mecoptera	Scorpion flies	9	550	Worldwide except Antarctica	Slender-winged insects that often have a curved abdomen. Adults feed on living insects, dead remains, or nectar. The larvae are often scavengers.
Siphonaptera	Fleas	18	2,000	Worldwide	Wingless parasitic insects that live on mammals and birds. Adults have flattened bodies for slipping through fur or feathers, and powerful back legs for jumping. Larvae are grublike and are scavengers.
Diptera	Two-winged flies	130	122,000	Worldwide	Insects with a single pair of wings and halteres. Adults have biting or sucking mouthparts, and feed mainly on liquid food, including nectar and blood. Fly larvae are wormlike. This order includes many parasites and pests.
Trichoptera	Caddis flies	43	8,000	Worldwide except Antarctica	Mothlike insects with slender antennae, usually found close to water. Caddis fly larvae live in water and often protect themselves by making portable cases.
Lepidoptera	Butterflies and moths	127	165,000	Worldwide except Antarctica	Insects whose bodies are completely covered with microscopic scales. Most butterflies and moths have broad wings, compact bodies, and tubular mouthparts that coil up when not in use.
Hymenoptera	Bees, wasps, and ants	91	198,000	Worldwide except Antarctica	Insects that typically have a "wasp waist" and two unequal pairs of wings. In flight, the forewings and hind wings are joined by microscopic hooks. Many species are armed with stings.

GLOSSARY

Abdomen The rear part of an insect's body, immediately behind its thorax. The abdomen contains an insect's reproductive system and also a large part of its digestive system.

Antenna (plural antennae) The feelers that most adult insects have on their heads. Insects use their antennae to smell, taste, and touch, and to feel vibrations in the air.

Anther A part of a flower that produces pollen. In many flowers, anthers are specially shaped so that they dust pollen onto visiting insects.

Anticoagulant A substance that stops blood from clotting when exposed to the air. Blood-sucking insects make anticoagulants and use them to keep blood flowing when they feed.

Arthropod An animal that has an exoskeleton, a segmented body, and legs with built-in joints. Arthropods include insects and many other invertebrates, such as spiders and centipedes.

Bacteria Single-celled microorganisms that are the simplest and most abundant living things on Earth. Bacteria live in all habitats, including on and inside other living things. Bacteria that cause disease are often known as germs.

Body case *See* exoskeleton

Camouflage Shapes, colors, and patterns that help insects and other animals to blend in with their surroundings.

Carnivore An animal that eats other animals as food.
See also predator

Carton A substance resembling cardboard that some termites use to make their nests. Termites make carton by chewing up dead wood.

Caste Specialized ranks in colony-forming insects, such as ants. In a colony, each caste has a different shape and does different work. Castes include workers, soldiers, and queens.

Cell A tiny unit of living matter, wrapped in an ultrathin membrane. An insect's body usually contains billions of cells, shaped to perform different tasks.

Cephalothorax In spiders and their relatives, the front part of the body. The cephalothorax consists of the head and thorax fused together.

Chromosomes Microscopic structures found in most living cells. Chromosomes contain the instructions (DNA) that are needed to build living things and make them work.

Chrysalis The pupa of a butterfly or moth. A chrysalis often has a hard and shiny outer case, but some are surrounded by silk cocoons.

Circulatory system In insects, the body system that pumps hemolymph around the body.

Classification A way of identifying and grouping living things. Scientific classification often helps to show how different living things are related through evolution.

Cocoon The silky protective case that some insects make just before they turn into a pupa.

Colony A group of insects that live together and that are all closely related. Most insect colonies are started by a single individual, called the queen.

Compound eye An eye that contains lots of separate units, each with its own lens.

Courtship A specialized kind of behavior that insects and other animals use to attract a mate, so that they can breed.

Coxa The uppermost part on an insect's leg, positioned next to its body. The coxa is attached to the thorax.

Crop Part of an insect's digestive system. The crop stores food before it is digested.

Digestive system The body system that breaks down food, and then absorbs the nutrients that it contains. The shape of an insect's digestive system varies according to the kind of food that it eats.

DNA Short for deoxyribonucleic acid. DNA is the substance that living things use to store information. It works like a chemical recipe, building cells and controlling how they work. *See also* chromosomes

Dormant Inactive for a long period of time. Insects become dormant so that they can survive difficult conditions.

Drone A male honey bee. Drones mate with queens, but unlike workers, they do not help to collect food or raise young.

Elytron (plural elytra) A beetle's forewings. Elytra are hard, and when they are closed, they fit over the hind wings like a case.

Entomologist A person who studies insects.

Evolution A slow change of the characteristics of living things, which results in their adjustment to the world around them. Instead of happening in a single lifetime, evolution takes place over several generations.

Exoskeleton A skeleton that covers the outside of an animal's body and protects the soft body parts underneath.

Eyespot A marking on an insect's wing that looks like a large eye. Insects use eyespots to scare away predators.

Family In scientific classification, a family is a group of species that are closely related.

Femur The part of an insect's leg that is directly above its knee. The femur is often the longest section of the leg.

Fertilization When living things reproduce, fertilization is the moment when a male cell and female cell come together. After fertilization, female insects lay their eggs.

Forewings In four-winged insects, the wings nearest the front of the thorax. The forewings are often thicker than the hind wings, and they protect the hind wings when they are closed.

Gall An abnormal growth in a plant that is triggered by an insect, mite, or sometimes by bacteria. Gall-forming insects use galls for shelter and for food.

Genes Chemical instructions that control the way living things grow, and the way they work. Genes are made from DNA, and they are passed on when living things reproduce.

Gills Organs that animals use to breathe underwater. In insects, gills collect oxygen and pass it to the tracheal system.

Grub A larva that has a short body without any legs. Most grubs move by wriggling or by chewing their way through their food.

Habitat The kind of surroundings that a living thing needs to survive. Most insects live in one sort of habitat and depend on it for survival.

Hemolymph The insect equivalent of blood. Unlike human blood, hemolymph is under low pressure, and it flows slowly through spaces in the body, instead of through arteries and veins.

Haltere In two-winged flies, a small pin-shaped organ that takes the place of the hind wings. Halteres help flies to balance when they are in the air.

Hibernation A deep winter sleep. By hibernating, insects can live through the coldest time of year without needing to find food.

Hind wings In four-winged insects, the wings nearest the rear of the thorax. The hind wings are often thinner than the forewings and may fold up many times before being stowed away.

Host An animal that is attacked by a parasite. The host is weakened by the parasite, but usually survives.

Hyperparasite Any parasite that attacks another parasite.

Invertebrate An animal that does not have a backbone or a bony skeleton. Invertebrates include insects and all other arthropods, as well as many other animals, particularly in freshwater and the sea. Invertebrates are often small, but they far outnumber vertebrates, and are much more varied.

Iridescent Reflecting light in a way that splits it into different colors. Iridescence is common in insects, and it often makes them look metallic.

Larva (plural larvae) A young insect that develops by complete metamorphosis. Larvae usually look completely different from their parents, and they often eat different food. They change into adults during a resting stage called a pupa.

Mask In young dragonflies and damselflies, a set of hinged mouthparts that can shoot out from under the head to catch other animals.

Metamorphosis A change in body shape as an insect or other animal grows up. Insects change shape in two ways. Those that develop by incomplete metamorphosis start life as nymphs, which look similar to their parents. They change slowly and gradually as they grow up. Those that develop by complete metamorphosis start life as larvae. They look very different to their parents, and they change abruptly during a resting stage, or pupa.

Migration A journey between two different parts of the world, to make use of different conditions at different times of year.

Mimic An insect that protects itself by looking like something that is inedible or dangerous to eat. Many insects mimic other insects that taste unpleasant, or that can bite or sting.

Molting Shedding the outer layer of the exoskeleton, so that the body can grow and change shape. In insects, molting is often known as "shedding the skin."

Nasute A specialized soldier termite with a head shaped like a nozzle. Nasutes squirt sticky substances at anything that attacks their nests.

Nectar A sugary liquid produced by flowers. Flowers make nectar to attract insect visitors, and they use insects to spread their pollen.

Nervous system The body system that senses the outside world and makes an insect move.

Nymph A young insect that develops by incomplete metamorphosis. Nymphs usually look similar to their parents, but they do not have wings. They change shape slightly each time they molt and develop working wings after the last molt, when they become adults.

Ocellus (plural ocelli) A simple eye on the top of an insect's head. Unlike a compound eye, an ocellus does not produce an image. Instead, it simply senses overall levels of light.

Order In scientific classification, an order is a major group of animals that contains one or more families. Insects in the same order are built in the same underlying way, although they often have very different body proportions and different ways of life.

Parasite An insect that lives on or inside another animal and that uses it as food.

Parasitoid An insect that starts life as a parasitic larva, feeding inside a host. By the time the parasitoid becomes adult, its host dies. Most insect parasitoids attack other insects.

Pheromone A substance given off by one insect that affects the behavior of another. Insects use pheromones to attract partners, to keep in touch, and to sound the alarm if their nests are attacked. Pheromones spread by direct contact or through the air.

Pollen A dustlike substance produced by flowers that contains the plant's male sex cells. Flowers have to exchange pollen before they can make their seeds.

Pollination The transfer of pollen from one flower to another. Some flowers are pollinated by the wind, but many use insects as pollen-carriers.

Predator An animal that hunts and eats others.

Prey An animal hunted by another for food.

Prolegs In caterpillars, short soft legs toward the rear of the body. Unlike true legs, prolegs do not have segments or joints.

Pupa (plural pupae) A resting stage in an insect's life cycle. During this stage, a larva's body is broken down and rebuilt to form an adult. Pupae are found only in insects that develop by complete metamorphosis.

Queen The founding female in an insect colony. In most colonies, the queen is the only colony member to lay eggs, and the workers are all her offspring.

Reproductive system The body system that enables insects to breed. In male insects, it produces sperm cells, and in most females, it produces eggs. Some females are able to breed without having to mate.

Reproductives In an insect colony, reproductives are males and females that fly off to form new nests of their own. Females that succeed in starting a nest become queens.

Resilin A very rubbery substance in insect bodies. Insects use resilin to store up energy, which helps them to jump or to fly.

Respiratory system The body system that carries oxygen to living cells and carries away carbon dioxide waste. In insects, the system consists of air-filled tubes called tracheae.

Rostrum Slender beak-shaped mouthparts that some insects use to pierce and suck up food.

Scavenger An insect or other animal that feeds on dead remains.

Segment A unit that makes up an insect's body. Segments are often visible in the exoskeleton. Each one has a collection of hard outer plates, separated from its neighbors by narrow joints.

Social insect An insect that lives with others in a colony. Social insects share the work involved in both feeding and breeding.

Soldier In insect colonies, soldiers are specialized workers that defend the nest or help to capture prey.

Species A group of living things that look similar and are capable of breeding together in the wild. A species is the basic unit that scientists use in classifying living things.

Spiracle A breathing hole on the surface of an insect's body. Spiracles allow air to flow into an insect's tracheae (breathing tubes).

Stigma A part of a flower that produces seeds. In many flowers, stigmas are specially shaped so that they collect pollen from visiting insects.

Sting A modified egg-laying tube that ants, bees, and wasps use to inject venom. They use stings to attack their prey, or for self-defense.

Stridulation A way of making sound by rubbing body parts together. Insects often stridulate with their legs or wings.

Surface tension An attractive force between water molecules that gives water a surface film. Some insects use surface tension to walk over ponds and streams.

Tarsus An insect's foot. The tarsus consists of several small segments and often ends in one or more claws.

Thorax The middle part of an insect's body, between the head and abdomen. The wings and legs are attached to the thorax, which contains most of the muscles that make them move.

Tibia The part of an insect's leg below its knee.

Trachea (plural tracheae) A tube that carries air into an insect's body, so that it can breathe. Tracheae start at openings called spiracles, and they divide into microscopic branches, which spread out to reach individual cells.

Venom A mixture of poisonous chemicals. Insects use venom to defend themselves, or to paralyze or kill their prey.

Vertebrate An animal with an internal skeleton.

Warning colors Bright colors that warn that an insect is dangerous or unpleasant to eat.

Worker An insect that lives in a colony and collects food, maintains the nest, and looks after the colony's young. Workers are usually female, but normally they do not breed.

INDEX

A page number in **bold** refers to the main entry for that subject.

ACKNOWLEDGMENTS

Dorling Kindersley would like to thank Lynn Bresler for proofreading and the index; Margaret Parrish for Americanization; and Niki Foreman for editorial assistance.

David Burnie would like to express his warm thanks to Dr. George McGavin for his help and advice during the preparation of this book, and also to Clare Lister of Dorling Kindersley, for her enthusiasm and expertise in bringing the book to completion.

Dorling Kindersley Ltd. is not responsible and does not accept liability for the availability or content of any Web site other than its own, or for any exposure to offensive, harmful, or inaccurate material that may appear on the Internet. Dorling Kindersley Ltd. will have no liability for any damage or loss caused by viruses that may be downloaded as a result of looking at and browsing the web sites that it recommends. Dorling Kindersley downloadable images are the sole copyright of Dorling Kindersley Ltd., and may not be reproduced, stored, or transmitted in any form or by any means for any commercial or profit-related purpose without prior written permission of the copyright owner.

Picture credits
The publisher would like to thank the following for their kind permission to reproduce their photographs:

Abbreviations key:
t-top, b-bottom, r-right, l-left, c-center, a-above, f-far

1 DK Images: Frank Greenaway c. 2 Science Photo Library: Claude Nuridsany & Marie Perennou c. 3 FLPA: Mark Moffett/Minden Pictures c. 4 Corbis: Lynda Richardson c. 7 DK Images: Dave King crb. 8 DK Images: Dave King cl; Jane Burton crb. 8 Warren Photographic: car. 8-9 Corbis: W. Cody. DK Images: Frank Greenaway. 9 Ardea.com: Pascal Goetgheluck cbr. 9 Corbis: Hyungwon Kang/Reuters cra. DK Images: Colin Keates bcl. Nature Picture Library Ltd: Duncan McEwan bcr; Nick Garbutt cr. 10 DK Images: Frank Greenaway cb; Geoff Dann clb; Kim Taylor cbr. Warren Photographic: bcl. 10-11 DK Images: Colin Keates. 11 Alamy Images: Nigel Cattlin/Agency Holt Studios International Ltd bcr. Corbis: Gary W. Carter br; George D.Lepp cr; Michael Clark/Frank Lane Picture Agency cfr. N.H.P.A.: Stephen Dalton tcr. Science Photo Library: Susumu Nishinaga cbl. Warren Photographic: tr. 12 Alamy Images: David Sanger tcr. Ardea.com: Alan Weaving cb. Corbis: Ralph A.Clevenger cr. DK Images: Frank Greenaway clb; Steven Wooster br. 13 Corbis: Carl & Ann Purcell bcl; Strauss/Curtis cbl. DK Images: Colin Keates cr, bcr; Francesca Yorke cra; Frank Greenaway tc, ca. 14 The Natural History Museum, London: ca. OSF/photolibrary.com: b. 15 Natural Visions: crb. DK Images: Dave King tr. FLPA: Michael & Patricia Fogden/Minden Pictures cfr. Science Photo Library: Claude Nuridsany & Marie Perennou cal; Eye of Science bcl; Vaughan Fleming bc. 16 Science Photo Library: Claude Nuridsany & Marie Perennou bl; Dr Jeremy Burgess clb. 17 Nature Picture Library Ltd: Hans

Christoph Kappel tr. N.H.P.A.: Ant Photo Library br. 18 Science Photo Library: Eye of Science clb, cfl; John Burbidge ca. 19 DK Images: Frank Greenaway cr, cb, crb; Kim Taylor cbr; Peter Anderson car, tcr. N.H.P.A.: George Bernard cbl. Science Photo Library: Claude Nuridsany & Marie Perennou cal, tcl. 20 N.H.P.A.: Stephen Dalton tcl. Getty Images: National Geographic bl. 20-21 Warren Photographic. 21 Ardea.com: John Mason bcl. Warren Photographic: br. Professor Dr. Ruediger Wehner: car. 22 DK Images: Frank Greenaway bl. N.H.P.A.: George Bernard tcr. 22-23 DK Images: Frank Greenaway. 23 Auscape: cfr. DK Images: Frank Greenaway bl, bc, br, crb. N.H.P.A.: Robert Thompson tcr. OSF/photolibrary.com: cbl. Warren Photographic: tc. 24 DK Images: Steve Gorton bl. 24-25 DK Images: Dave King. 25 Alamy Images: Nigel Cattlin/Holt Studios International Ltd cbr; Wildchromes tr. DK Images: Jerry Young crb. Science Photo Library: Claude Nuridsany & Marie Perennou tc. Warren Photographic: car. 26 DK Images: Colin Keates/The Natural History Museum, London bcr; Frank Greenaway crb; Kim Taylor tl, cla, bl. 27 DK Images: Steve Gorton t. N.H.P.A.: Alan Barnes bcl. Warren Photographic: br. 28-29 Warren Photographic. 29 DK Images: Colin Keates car; Dave King cfr; Frank Greenaway car; Frank Greenaway/The Natural History Museum, London cra; Steve Gorton tc. N.H.P.A.: Stephen Dalton cl. Warren Photographic: tl. 30-31 DK Images: Frank Greenaway. 31 Alamy Images: Maximilian Weinzierl tl; NaturePicks car. DK Images: Neil Fletcher br, tcr. N.H.P.A.: Stephen Dalton cbr. OSF/photolibrary.com: ca. Science Photo Library: Andy Harmer cr. 32 DK Images: Frank Greenaway clb, cfl. Nature Picture Library Ltd: Martin Dohrn cr. 32-33 DK Images: Frank Greenaway. 33 Michael and Patricia Fogden: crb. Nature Picture Library Ltd: Premaphotos cfr. 34 Natural Visions: bl. Corbis: Clouds Hill Imaging Ltd cb. DK Images: Neil Fletcher ca. Science Photo Library: Claude Nuridsany & Marie Perennou car. 34-35 DK Images: Neil Fletcher. 35 DK Images: Neil Fletcher tl, c, br. N.H.P.A.: M.I. Walker tr. OSF/photolibrary.com: ca. 36 Corbis: Michael & Patricia Fogden bl. OSF/photolibrary.com: cra, bcr. 36-37 OSF/photolibrary.com. 37 N.H.P.A.: George Bernard cl. OSF/photolibrary.com: cla, br. Warren Photographic: car, tcr. 38 DK Images: Geoff Brightling/Peter Minster car. Nature Picture Library Ltd: Martin Dohrn b. 39 DK Images: Steve Gorton/Oxford Museum of Natural History tl. Science Photo Library: Dr Gary Gaugler bl; John Burbidge cfl; Sinclair Stammers cla, crb. Warren Photographic: cra, car. 40 DK Images: Frank Greenaway cbr; Kim Taylor cbl. OSF/photolibrary.com: clb, cb. 41 N.H.P.A.: Stephen Dalton cfr. OSF/photolibrary.com: tr. Science Photo Library: Eye of Science ca; Sinclair Stammers crb. Warren Photographic: tl. 42 Corbis: Gary W. Carter bl. Science Photo Library: bcr; J.C.Revy cb; VVG ca. 43 DK Images: Frank Greenaway br; Steve Gorton cbl. Nature Picture Library Ltd: Premaphotos tcl. Science Photo Library: Claude Nuridsany & Marie Perennou cbr. FLPA: Minden Pictures clb. Nature Picture Library Ltd: Premaphotos tl. Science Photo Library: Darwin Dale/Agstock cb. 45 DK Images: Kim Taylor cbl. N.H.P.A.: Stephen Dalton cb. Science Photo

Library: Claude Nuridsany & Marie Perennou tr; Michael Abbey cal. 46 DK Images: Oxford Scientific Films b. Science Photo Library: Susumu Nishinaga tl. 47 DK Images: Howard Rice cb; Kim Taylor tr. N.H.P.A.: Robert Thompson tl. Warren Photographic: clb, cfr. 48 Ardea.com: D.W.Greenslade cfl. DK Images: Neil Fletcher cfl. N.H.P.A.: Stephen Dalton bl. OSF/photolibrary.com: bcr. Warren Photographic: clb. 48-49 N.H.P.A.: James Carmichael JR. 49 Corbis: David A. Northcott tr. N.H.P.A.: Stephen Dalton tcl. Science Photo Library: Darwin Dale/Agstock ca. 50 DK Images: Gables cfl. Warren Photographic: car. 50-51 N.H.P.A.: Anthony Bannister. 51 DK Images: Steve Gorton/Oxford University Museum cfr. The Natural History Museum, London: cbr. N.H.P.A.: Stephen Dalton tr. 52 DK Images: Frank Greenaway/The Natural History Museum, London car. Nature Picture Library Ltd: Ingo Arndt tr. 53 DK Images: Frank Greenaway crb. Holt Studios International: ca. N.H.P.A.: Anthony Bannister cfl. OSF/photolibrary.com: bc, br, bcr. 54 DK Images: Colin Keates/The Natural History Museum, London clb; Jerry Young bl. 54-55 N.H.P.A.: Anthony Bannister. 55 Natural Visions: bcl. DK Images: Frank Greenaway tr, cr, cbl; Frank Greenaway/The Natural History Museum, London c, tc; Harry Taylor/The Natural History Museum, London br. N.H.P.A.: Stephen Dalton crb. 56 N.H.P.A.: Daniel Heuclin clb. 56-57 Warren Photographic. 57 Alamy: Ashok Captain/Agency Ephotocorp crb. DK Images: Colin Keates tcr; Frank Greenaway tc, tr. FLPA: tcl. Getty Images: Taxi c. 58 Corbis: Galen Rowell tr. Warren Photographic: b. 59 Ardea.com: Steve Hopkin br. Holt Studios International: t. Nature Picture Library Ltd: cl; Richard Bowsher c. Warren Photographic: bcl. 60 Alamy Images: Maximilian Weinzierl cfl. FLPA: Mitsuhiko Imamori/Minden Pictures b. N.H.P.A.: Eric Soder tr. 61 DK Images: Frank Greenaway tl; Jane Burton br. FLPA: Michael & Patricia Fogden/Minden Pictures clb, bl, cfl. N.H.P.A.: Daniel Heuclin tr. 62 Nature Picture Library Ltd: Hans Christoph Kappel cfl. 62 OSF/photolibrary.com: bl. 62-63 Science Photo Library: Andrew Syred. 63 Ardea.com: cr. DK Images: Frank Greenaway br; Kim Taylor cfr. N.H.P.A.: Anthony Bannister bc. OSF/photolibrary.com: tr. 64 Corbis: Michael & Patricia Fogden. DK Images: Neil Fletcher bl, bc, bcl. 64-65 DK Images: Linda Whitwam; Neil Fletcher. 65 Natural Visions: cbr. Ardea.com: bcr; Alan Weaving cr. DK Images: Frank Greenaway cbr; Neil Fletcher cl. Ecoscene: tcr. Nature Picture Library Ltd: car; Robin Chittenden cra. N.H.P.A.: Gerry Cambridge tcr. 66 DK Images: Andy Crawford/Gary Stabb - modelmaker bcl; Dave King c, cfl; Frank Greenaway cb; Jane Burton bl; Kim Taylor br. N.H.P.A.: John Shaw tc, tr. 67 Corbis: Roy Morsch br. DK Images: Frank Greenaway cl; Frank Greenaway/The Natural History Museum, London cl; Kim Taylor c. Nature Picture Library Ltd: Ingo Arndt bl. N.H.P.A.: John Shaw tl, tc, tr. Jerry Young tr; Ted Benton crb. 68-69 DK Images: Kim Taylor and Jane Burton. 69 Corbis: Pat Jerrold/Papilio tcr. DK Images: Jerry Young tr; Ted Benton crb. FLPA: Mitsuhiko Imamoril/Minden Pictures cfr. OSF/photolibrary.com: cl. 70 Ardea.com: cla. DK Images: Frank Greenaway cbr, cfl; Kim Taylor cl; Steve Gorton/Oxford University Museum c.

OSF/photolibrary.com: bl. Warren Photographic: cr. 70-71 FLPA: Mitsuhiko Imamori/Minden Pictures. 71 Ardea.com: cbr; Steve Hopkin cra. FLPA: Mitsuhiko Imamori/Minden Pictures crb. Nature Picture Library Ltd: David Welling bc. 72 Corbis: Michael T. Sedam b; Wolfgang Kaehler car. 73 Natural Visions: tl. Ardea.com: John Mason br; Steve Hopkin cla. DK Images: Frank Greenaway car; Guy Ryecart/The Ivy Press Limited cfr. FLPA: Fritz Polking cbl. 74 DK Images: Frank Greenaway cla, clb, cfl. Nature Picture Library Ltd: Andrew Cooper br; Pete Oxford bl; Premaphotos bc. 74-75 DK Images: Oxford Scientific Film. 75 Ardea.com: Alan Weaving bc. Nature Picture Library Ltd: Hermann Brehm bl; Martin Dohrn br. 76-77 DK Images: Frank Greenaway. 77 DK Images: Geoff Dann bcl. Nature Picture Library Ltd: John B Free tcl. OSF/photolibrary.com: tc. Warren Photographic: br. 78 DK Images: Kim Taylor c. 78-79 DK Images: Kim Taylor. Warren Photographic. 79 Natural Visions: crb. Ardea.com: Steve Hopkin car. DK Images: Frank Greenaway cbl. N.H.P.A.: Anthony Bannister crb; Stephen Dalton cb. OSF/photolibrary.com: cbr. 80 DK Images: Jerry Young c. Warren Photographic: cla. 80-81 N.H.P.A.: Manfred Danegger. 81 Natural Visions: tl. FLPA: Konrad Wothe/Minden Pictures bcr; Treat Davidson car. Nature Picture Library Ltd: Premaphotos tcr. N.H.P.A.: N.A. Callow cbr; Steve Robinson cr. Science Photo Library: B.G Thomson cbl. 82 Science Photo Library: Sinclair Stammers tr, c. 82-83 FLPA: Mitsuhiko Imamori/Minden Pictures. 83 Nature Picture Library Ltd: John Cancalosi br. N.H.P.A.: Eric Soder tr; Martin Harvey tl. Science Photo Library: David Scharf cfr. 84 Holt Studios International: bl. OSF/photolibrary.com: cl. 84-85 FLPA: Frans Lanting/Minden Pictures. 85 Jeffrey A. Lockwood: br, cbr. 86 Corbis: Michael Pole bl; Wolfgang Kaehler cra. 87 Alamy Images: Steve Fallon/Agency LifeFile Photos Ltd cl. Corbis: Naturfoto Honal tc. DK Images: Frank Greenaway cr. N.H.P.A.: Daniel Heuclin tr. Science Photo Library: Jack K. Clark/Agstock tr; Peter Menzel bcl. 88 Ardea.com: tr. 88-89 Science Photo Library: Peter Menzel. 89 ASA-Multimedia: Thomas Kujawski tb. 89 DK Images: Colin Keates br; Nigel Hicks car. The Natural History Museum, London: crb. N.H.P.A.: Ant Photo Library tr. Eric Preston: cfr. Science Photo Library: Debra Ferguson/Agstock tcl. 92 DK Images: Frank Greenaway l. 93 DK Images: Frank Greenaway r. 94 DK Images: Frank Greenaway l. 95 DK Images: Frank Greenaway r. 96 DK Images: Frank Greenaway l.

Jacket images
Front: Getty Images: J.H. Pete Carmichael (ccr); Gary Vestal (ccl). National Geographic Image Collection: Tim Laman (cl). Science Photo Library: Andrew Syred (cr).
Back: Getty Images: Charles Krebs (ccl); David Maitland (ccr). National Geographic Image Collection: Robert Sisson (cl). OSF/photolibrary.com: Olivier Grunewald (cl).

All other images © Dorling Kindersley.
For further information see:
www.dkimages.com